THE FUTURE OF
RECRUITMENT

These leading experts in assessment and technology generously share their insights on the new frontier of talent management tools driven by AI (e.g., video interviews, resume screening, game-based assessments). Authors also raise critically important attendant issues regarding privacy, algorithmic bias, and other legal and ethical concerns. The book stands to contribute to fruitful multidisciplinary collaborations, challenging conversations, and productive disagreements essential to meaningful advances in this domain.

–Dr Fred Oswald, Professor and Herbert S. Autrey Chair in Social Sciences, Department of Psychological Sciences and Management, Rice University

This book not only describes recruitment technology in a way that is both easy to understand and rich in scientific detail, it also captures the ethical and societal consequences of recruitment. One of the most important books on recruitment to read.

–Frida Polli, CEO and Cofounder of Pymetrics

Everything that's important to know about the future of recruitment is put together in this engaging book which will impact the way we think about recruitment for years to come. New and emerging recruitment technology is expertly captured, if you want to understand the science underlying today's and tomorrow's recruitment tech, look no further.

–Michal Kosinski, Associate Professor of Organizational Behavior, Stanford Graduate School of Business

The Future of Work

The future of work is a vital contemporary area of debate both in business and management research, and in wider social, political, and economic discourse. Globally relevant issues, including the aging workforce, rise of the gig economy, workplace automation, and changing forms of business ownership, are all regularly the subject of discussion in both academic research and the mainstream media, having wider professional and public policy implications.

The Future of Work series features books examining key issues or challenges in the modern workplace, synthesizing prior developments in critical thinking, alongside current practical challenges in order to interrogate possible future developments in the world of work.

Offering future research agendas and suggesting practical outcomes for today's and tomorrow's businesses and workforce, the books in this series present powerful, challenging, and polemical analysis of a diverse range of subjects in their potential to address future challenges and possible new trajectories.

The series highlights what changes still need to be made to core areas of business practice and theory in order for them to be forward-facing, more representative, and able to fulfill the industrial challenges of the future.

Algorithms, Blockchain and Cryptocurrency: Implications for the Future of the Workplace

Gavin Brown and Richard Whittle

HR without People? Industrial Evolution in the Age of Automation, AI, and Machine Learning

Anthony R. Wheeler and Ronald M. Buckley

The Healthy Workforce: Enhancing Wellbeing and Productivity in the Workers of the Future

Stephen Bevan and Cary L. Cooper

FORTHCOMING TITLES

Spending Without Thinking: The Future of Consumption

Richard Whittle

Cooperatives at Work

George Cheney, Matt Noyes and Emi Do

THE FUTURE OF RECRUITMENT

Using the New Science of Talent Analytics to Get Your Hiring Right

BY

FRANZISKA LEUTNER
Goldsmiths, University of London, UK

REECE AKHTAR
Deeper Signals, USA

And

TOMAS CHAMORRO-PREMUZIC
University College London, UK

United Kingdom – North America – Japan – India
Malaysia – China

Emerald Publishing Limited
Howard House, Wagon Lane, Bingley BD16 1WA, UK

First edition 2022

Reprints and permissions service
Contact: permissions@emeraldinsight.com

British Library Cataloguing in Publication Data
A catalogue record for this book is available from the British Library

ISBN: 978-1-83867-562-2 (Print)
ISBN: 978-1-83867-559-2 (Online)
ISBN: 978-1-83867-561-5 (Epub)

ISOQAR certified
Management System,
awarded to Emerald
for adherence to
Environmental
standard
ISO 14001:2004.

Certificate Number 1985
ISO 14001

INVESTOR IN PEOPLE

CONTENTS

ABOUT THE AUTHORS

Dr Franziska Leutner is a Lecturer in Occupational Psychology at Goldsmiths College, University of London. She is an organizational psychologist and data scientist and publishes scientific articles on computational psychometrics, game-based assessments, personality, and entrepreneurship. As a product innovator, she has worked with tech companies and startups to develop the next generation of assessment and selection tools, including at HireVue where she is currently Director of Assessment Innovation. She holds a PhD from University College London, where she was a lecturer for several years.

Dr Reece Akhtar is a Cofounder and CEO of Deeper Signals. He is an organizational psychologist and data scientist specializing in applied personality assessment and computational psychometrics. As a lecturer at NYU and researcher at UCL, he has published scientific articles on personality, talent management, leadership, entrepreneurship, and machine learning. Previously he led product innovation at RHR International and Hogan Assessments Systems.

Dr Tomas Chamorro-Premuzic is an international authority in psychological profiling, talent management, leadership development, and people analytics. His commercial work focuses on the creation of science-based tools that improve organizations' ability to predict performance and people's ability to understand themselves. He is currently the Chief Talent Scientist at ManpowerGroup, Cofounder of Deeper Signals and Metaprofiling, and Professor of Business Psychology at University College London and Columbia University. He has previously held academic positions at New York University and the London School of Economics, and frequently lectures at Harvard Business School, Stanford Business School, London Business School, and IMD, as well as being the former CEO at Hogan Assessment Systems. Find out more here: www.drtomas.com.

1

THE PAST, PRESENT, AND FUTURE OF RECRUITMENT

The three of us have been fascinated by the study of recruitment for some time now. The reason is simple: humans spend a big proportion of their adult life at work, and the difference between picking the right or the wrong career has significant financial, emotional, and health consequences (Laspita, Breugst, Heblich, & Patzelt, 2012). When we make good career choices we thrive, find meaning, and not only apply our natural talents and skills, but also develop our full potential (Lu, Wang, Lu, Du, & Bakker, 2014). In contrast, when we make poor career decisions, we end up bored, alienated, and stressed, and our talents will simply go to waste (Maslach, Schaufeli, & Leiter, 2001). J.K. Rowling was on unemployment benefits after a lackluster career as a teacher when she finally found her niche as a children's author – to become the most successful author of all time. Brad Pitt was a limo driver, Pope Francis a nightclub bouncer, and Whoopi Goldberg a funeral make-up artist. These are just famous examples of people who started their lives in the wrong careers, but were at least lucky, courageous, and persistent enough to change. In

contrast, many people end up stuck in unfulfilling or mean-
ingless jobs, highlighting the importance of picking the right
career to begin with. Unsurprisingly, there are obvious parallels between a happy career and a happy relationship, just
like there are clear parallels between an unhappy career and
an unhappy relationship (Ahmetoglu, Swami, & Chamorro-
Premuzic, 2010), but it is likely that people are more likely to
put up with a bad career than a bad relationship, and not for
lack of choices.

An even bigger reason we are passionate about recruitment
is that we are psychologists, and as our own research and
careers have taught us, there's a robust body of psychological
knowledge and science to significantly increase the probability
that every individual ends up in the right career, maximizing
the fit between their unique dispositions, interests, and talents,
and the particular requirements of the job or career they pick
(Chamorro-Premuzic & Furnham, 2010). This specific area of
psychology has resulted in a prolific field of research within
Industrial-Organizational Psychology for over a century, and
its results is the equivalent of a Cupid or Match.com for
careers (Kanfer, Ackerman, Murtha, & Goff, 1995). Imagine
a proven science that is able to help us understand and predict
what each person is good at, how they differ from others, and
what they are able to do better than their peers, combined
with the ability to find a perfect home for their strengths and
talents so that they end up fulfilled and happy in their careers.
Confucius allegedly noted that if you pick a job you love you
will never work a day in your life – he was right, but in today's
complex world, this requires a fair bit of expertise and science,
not to mention reliable tools and a rigorous methodology.

In a nutshell, that's what we do for a living: we are like a
Cupid for careers, and our methods are grounded in a century
of psychological research that explains why you like certain
jobs but dislike others, why you are good at some things but

not great at others, and what that implies for your career and professional choices (Chamorro-Premuzic, 2017). Recruitment is the broad industry that brings it all together, because recruiters search and match with the objective of helping organizations find the right person for the right job, as well as help humans find the right job – and ideally career – for their own unique skills, personalities, and interests. When we don't intervene you get what usually happens: people making random career choices based on what their aunt or uncle suggested, or what their parents prescribe: "why don't you go be a doctor like your godfather", or "why don't you study IT, so you can make good money?" In the realm of relationships this equates to marrying someone after a drunken encounter at a bar, or on the basis of a prearranged marriage, but with lower probability of success. Yes, prearranged marriages often outlasts "free" or self-determined marriages, not least because divorce rates in the rich world hover around 50%, so the bar is quite low, but there is still a much better way to get matched, both in the realm of love and work: namely, understand who you really are, and where your talents and potential are best deployed (Chamorro-Premuzic, 2016).

In that sense, there's a clear evolution in the world of careers, which explains why recruitment has become very data-driven and psychological in the past few decades. For most of our evolutionary history, including modern civilizations, our career success and professional fates were determined mostly by our *social capital*, a politically correct or oxymoronic way to talk about contacts and nepotism: *who you know* has usually explained where you end up, and how far in life you can go (Dillon, 2014). Alas, this is not quite obsolete in the twenty-first century, as privilege and status are more often inherited than acquired. But a big transformation began to occur with the advent of mainstream college education, and the rise of the creative classes: indeed, around 100

years ago or so what started to matter more than who you
know or social capital was intellectual capital or *what you
know* (Rindermann & Thompson, 2011). Enter the age of
credentials and hard skills, which explains the rise of qualifications, and the advent of the knowledge economy. This is still
the reason why a college degree is the main differentiator
between lower and higher paid jobs, and why so many people
in the world decide to take loans and debts in order to
upgrade their professional choices – unless they are elite ath-
letes, self-made entrepreneurs, or aristocrats, though university credentials are far from unusual in any of these groups.

And yet, there is clear consensus today on the idea that
college credentials, including Ivy League qualifications, are a
poor indicator of what people can do, not to mention the
realization that what you have learned in school and college is
far less important than what you can learn. Welcome to the
age of *psychological capital* (Luthans & Youssef-Morgan,
2017), where what matters most is not who you know or
what you know, but who you are. It is in this context that
organizations and employers everywhere have the urge to
understand people's values, abilities, and personalities. This
urge is an attempt to make the world of work more talent-
centric and meritocratic, aligning people's potential and talents with their jobs and careers, and coincides with an
unprecedented attempt to look for talent beyond the obvious
places, a major tenet underpinning the desire to build and
harness a diverse workforce.

Diversity and inclusion have never mattered as much as
now, and they will continue to raise in importance (Roberge &
van Dick, 2010). The implication of this is obvious: organizations, and particularly the top employers in the world, are
fighting a very specific battle in the war for talent – to identify
the *rare find*, and be able to source top talent from unusual and
unconventional places. Gone is the quest to hire for "culture

fit", which results in going to the same schools, tribes, and geographies, and a homogeneous talent pool that defaults to one dimensional beliefs and attitudes to create groupthink and kill creativity. If you really want to hire on culture fit, you may end up not with a culture, but with a cult. Today's top employers want *culture-add*, which means leveraging the distributed wisdom of the knowledge economy and harnessing the cognitive and psychological diversity that a wide range of individuals can produce when they have different backgrounds and perspectives (Wille, De Fruyt, Dingemanse, & Vergauwe, 2015). Within this context the future of recruitment will need to address a significant psychological challenge underpinning the science of people at work, namely understanding how to unlock and harness human potential.

Today, however, this is still the exception rather than the norm. In fact, we live in a world where most people are still misunderstood, especially by their employers, and even by themselves. How can you pick a rewarding and fulfilling career if you don't really know what you are good at? And how can employers hire you for the right job, if they don't really understand what you are good at? This is the challenge that excites us, and keeps us up at night. It is the problem we have dedicated our own professional lives to solving, and we are privileged and lucky for having made this choice: because we love what we do, and do what we love. Our dream is that every person in the world has the ability to make equivalent choices, and go into a field or job that they deeply care about and love. In order to achieve this, we need to bring the science of recruitment to life, ensuring it touches every single employer and organization in the world, and also do our bit to inform and perhaps even "nudge" the wide range of job applicants who could improve their choices if they understood themselves and their potential career options better. To be sure, we can't offer definitive answers to ensure a perfect match, but we can still improve both employers' and employees' decisions by sharing the insights of a well-established science on how to select the right person for the right job, and help people pick the right jobs for their own talents and passions.

Our focus with this book is on the future – because there is lots of room for improvement, and because we are living at an exciting moment in time. A time in which we can witness a promising convergence between a mature science of organizational psychology and scalable technologies for bringing this science to life, and making it a reality. This convergence is the result of ubiquitous individual and organizational data (Winsborough & Chamorro-Premuzic, 2013), and the ability to interpret these data in psychological terms to ensure that both organizations and employees can systematically bolster their understanding of talent and potential (Atkinson, Bench-Capon, & Bollegala, 2020). The better you know yourself, and the better potential employers know you, the more likely it is that you end up in the right career. Conversely, if you misunderstand your talents and live in a world in which organizations don't understand your talents and potential, you will only end up in the right career by accident. So, our job is to look to existing and emerging technologies in conjunction with the established science to improve the state of affairs for both employers and employees. In that sense, this book is an attempt to answer one major question: in what ways will organizations be able to select the best possible people for each job in the near future? To this end, we will try to distil the wide range of available innovations in this area – and assess what methods and tools may emerge in the next years – to depict the possibilities, opportunities, and risks for the future of recruitment.

The goal of this book is not so much to predict what *will* happen, but to prescribe – or at minimum recommend – what *should* or *ought to*. Our starting point is a fairly firm conviction that many of the common habits underpinning current practices are far from accurate, useful, or fair, and in many instances biased and corrupt (Chamorro-Premuzic, 2017). Indeed, we see the future as moving us from a relatively serendipitous and obsolete state of mainstream recruitment practices to a much more advanced point in the evolution of this industry where scientific and evidence-based decisions are relatively common, and where technology will play a big part: capturing the data that provides the raw materials for the science-based insights. To be sure, this will only happen if we can ensure that technologies, particularly AI and machine learning algorithms, are deployed in an ethical and moral way, such that they have a benevolent and beneficial impact for both workers and their employers (Fleming, 2021). We know this is certainly not a given, but we also know it is the only way in which organizations will gain a competitive advantage in the war for talent. Anywhere in the world, in-demand workers and sought-after talent will prefer to join organizations in which they are appreciated for what they contribute, understood and valued for whom they are, where politics and nepotism play a marginal role compared to meritocracy, and where the culture rewards moral and pro-social behaviors while sanctioning toxic acts. These principles ought to apply not just to humans but the technologies they deploy to make decisions. And while we cannot expect machines to have the moral conscience that propels them to act in ethical ways, we must hold humans accountable for unethical uses of technology, including AI.

In the next chapter, we shall highlight some of the specific ways in which this revolution may be achieved. While recent years have seen a great deal of innovation and activity in the space of HR technologies (Stone, Deadrick, Lukaszewski, & Johnson, 2015), which includes a wide range of efforts to disrupt and improve the recruitment industry, we identify some major themes and areas of innovation that have already reached a certain level of maturity and had significant and salient impact on either practices, science, or both. More specifically, the next chapters comprise:

Chapter 2: The data science revolution: An overview of how the digital age, combined with advances in AI and machine learning algorithms, have turbocharged the old science of personnel selection (Yarkoni & Westfall, 2017). This is where I-O psychology meets AI to offer a new range of talent "signals" to understand and predict people's potential and talent for different careers, and even help us infer whether someone is a good candidate for a job they have never done before, such as management and leadership roles. This field has advanced so quickly that it is hard to predict where it will end up – but we will highlight some of the more promising areas for development and application.

Chapter 3: Digital interviews: An overview of how technology platforms are replacing the most common historical method for vetting and selecting talent, namely the job interview (Suen, Chen, & Lu, 2019). While we have known for decades that typical interviews suffer from poor reliability and validity, and that the most accurate and reliable selection interviews are highly standardized and structured, to the point of resembling a controlled experiment or psychometric assessment, it was highly cumbersome and expensive for organizations to follow such rigorous processes. But, as we show in this chapter, the advent of the digital age, with ubiquitous video interviewing platforms and the vast corresponding data they capture – including voice, speech, body language, and language use – enables AI to detect hidden signals of potential while ignoring noise, including sensitive demographic information such as gender and race (which humans cannot ignore or unlearn).

Chapter 4: Social media analytics/digital profiling: An overview of how the sea of data we produce everyday, and the ocean of personal data that we produced in the past decade alone, could be translated into meaningful and accurate profiles of our skills, talent, and potential. Although this area has proven quite controversial for HR and recruiters to apply, not least after the Cambridge Analytica fiasco, it has fueled hundreds of scientific studies and represents the most prolific area of research around innovations in assessment and selection techniques (Lambiotte & Kosinski, 2014), largely inspired by digital marketing advances (Matz, Kosinski, Nave, & Stillwell, 2017). There is now so much data on everyone that the idea of assessing people by giving them a new tool or instrument is hard to justify, except for the non-trivial fact that such data are hard to retrieve, ethically and legally problematic to use, and of variable quality. Still, we see a future in which individuals may have access to the data they produced – perhaps even own it – and ethical AI can help them stitch it together to translate it into a valid talent passport, which potential employers and recruiters may scrutinize to determine person-role fit.

Chapter 5: Gamification and game-based assessments: An overview of how selection tools have evolved to take into consideration the candidate experience. Historically, job seekers were forced to complete long and tedious tests, in order to be considered for a job. Their experience didn't count, and if they didn't like it, they could simply decide to not apply or find a job elsewhere. But in an age where most top employers want to offer employees consumer-like experiences, and the recruitment process has been co-opted by employers marketing and branding functions, organizations are serious about creating the right type of engagement and branding experience even with prospective employees. This, together with innovations in tech and data science, explain the rise of gamification (Baptista & Oliveira, 2019): an attempt to apply game-like features to assessment tools so that they enhance candidates' experience, and hopefully increase the number of job applications (rather than deterring potential candidates). Game-like assessments now exist for all major competencies or attributes underpinning talent, and the main advancement in this area has been to significantly shorten assessment time so that boredom and fatigue are rare, and candidates have a seamless and fun experience when they apply for jobs.

Chapter 6: The ethics of future recruitment tools: An overview of the principles and rules that *ought to be applied* and respected, so that new innovations and technologies are deployed in ways that truly benefit candidates, protecting their data and anonymity, and creating a transparent and open relationship between employers and potential employees characterized by respect, informed consent, and a strict adherence to employment right laws (Fleming, 2021). Much has been written recently in the field of ethical AI and while it is true that we are still trying to hit a moving target, and that regulations are still evolving and to some degree playing catch up with advances in this space, there are also many strong rules and principles that have protected job applicants from unethical and illegal recruitment practices for decades, and which are largely still valid to regulate the often controversial and delicate space between what organizations could and should know about candidates, and minimize the asymmetry between what organizations want to know and need to know. Ultimately, the reputation of employers will rest on their ability to mitigate the risks that may emerge from misusing new technologies and failing to protect job applicants when they engage them in the recruitment process.

Chapter 7: The far future: An overview of possibilities if some of the more adventurous and experimental current trends were to crystalize or consolidate in the future. Science fiction accounts of a brave new world in which tech and AI account for a great chunk of automated decisions pertaining people's careers have long scared us, and there's no question that even recent fictional shows or technological dystopias, such as Black Mirror, are disturbingly close to reality. While some of these scenarios are indeed scary, we highlight many opportunities for advancements and improvements, including a more ethical and fair world of recruitment, courtesy of these possible innovations. With these examples we seek to inspire ethical organizations to try to experiment with far neglected tools in the hope of improving their own processes and systems, and advancing progress in the war for talent. We also note that employees and job seekers could be better off if these futuristic alternatives become a reality.

A final note concerning you, dear reader. In writing this book, we envisaged that you may fit into one of these three categories, and perhaps even more than one at once:

• You are responsible for evaluating and selecting talent, either in your own organization or as an independent recruiter acting in the service of others. The former includes being a manager, boss, or supervisor and having to decide whether you hire someone or not, as well as being part of the HR function, especially talent acquisition. In any of these cases you will be more interested in the practical aspects of emerging technologies and tools in the field of recruitment, so that you can decide what tools may be useful for you, and have a relatively strong sense of whether something is robust or not. While we don't expect you to go deep into the science, we will try to distill and simplify the practical aspects of the tools we review, so you can leverage them in your professional practice.

- You are researching emerging trends in the recruitment industry, perhaps as a journalist, HR management student, or Industrial-Organizational Psychology scholar. This may mean that you have some knowledge and expertise in traditional HR or human capital, but are interested in understanding how technology and data-fueled innovations may be changing, if not advancing or disrupting, the field. In this case, you will be interested in some of the research close-ups we offer when we highlight the growing academic and peer-reviewed research studies at the intersection of AI, psychology, and talent management. Most large organizations have created their own people analytics teams (sometimes even departments), with PhD level data scientists who are focused on bridging the practice-science gap in recruitment. If you are in this category we are happy to count you as a fellow data-geek, and will try to provide sufficient ammunition to nourish your hungry mind.

- You are just a curious person, interested in understanding the complex world of careers, and how organizations may be advancing their ability to understand your talent and potential. This may also include a more practical or concrete interest in preparing yourself for future job searchers, and the desire to be as informed as you can about the tools and methods companies deploy – and should deploy – when you express an interest in joining them. This may also mean you are interested in developing your career within your current organization, so you want to understand what data and insights your employer may have on you, and how that will impact your ability to move up or progress in that system. While our book is not designed to help you perform well on any of the innovations we highlight, we hope to include sufficient information that you extract some useful personal learnings, and that you feel more equipped when you think about what your data says about you, how to curate a desirable professional reputation, and how to increase your own career-related self-awareness. In short, we would love to help you understand your own talents and potential through some of the advances we discuss in this book.

Whichever category describes you best, it is our hope that you approach this book with an open and critical mind. Be as skeptical as you can, question what you read, and put whatever we say to the test of your own logic and common sense, as well as inspecting the sources and materials we use as evidence. Science is never about the ultimate way of being right, but rather finding better ways of being wrong. In that sense, we see this book as an incomplete analyses and take of what we regard as the more reliable and trustworthy research in this field: it is neither definitive nor conclusive, but rather indicative and compelling. The new science of recruitment is very young and still very much a work in progress, so our only hope is that this book will enhance the efforts of those who attempt to carefully put it to practice to improve both organizations' success and people's careers.

REFERENCES

Ahmetoglu, G., Swami, V., & Chamorro-Premuzic, T. (2010). The relationship between dimensions of love, personality, and relationship length. *Archives of Sexual Behavior*, *39*(5), 1181–1190. doi:10.1007/s10508-009-9515-5

Atkinson, K., Bench-Capon, T., & Bollegala, D. (2020). Explanation in AI and law: Past, present and future. *Artificial Intelligence*, *289*, 103387. doi:10.1016/j.artint.2020.103387

Baptista, G., & Oliveira, T. (2019). Gamification and serious games: A literature meta-analysis and integrative model. *Computers in Human Behavior*, *92*, 306–315. doi:10.1016/j.chb.2018.11.030

Chamorro-Premuzic, T. (2016). What science tells us about leadership potential. Retrieved from https://hbr.org/2016/09/what-science-tells-us-about-leadership-potential

Chamorro-Premuzic, T. (2017). *The talent delusion: Why data, not intuition, is the key to unlocking human potential*. London: Piatkus.

Chamorro-Premuzic, T., & Furnham, A. (2010). *The psychology of personnel selection*. Cambridge: Cambridge University Press. doi:10.1037/h0052197

Dillon, K. (2014). *HBR guide to office politics*. Boston, MA: Harvard Business Review Press.

Fleming, M. N. (2021). Considerations for the ethical implementation of psychological assessment through social media via machine learning. *Ethics & Behavior*, *31*(3), 181–192. doi:10.1080/10508422.2020.1817026

Kanfer, R., Ackerman, P. L., Murtha, T., & Goff, M. (1995). Personality and intelligence in industrial and organizational psychology. In *International handbook of personality and intelligence* (pp. 577–602). Boston, MA: Springer US. doi:10.1007/978-1-4757-5571-8_26

Lambiotte, R., & Kosinski, M. (2014). Tracking the digital footprints of personality. *Proceedings of the IEEE*, *102*(12), 1934–1939. doi:10.1109/JPROC.2014.2359054

Laspita, S., Breugst, N., Heblich, S., & Patzelt, H. (2012). Intergenerational transmission of entrepreneurial intentions. *Journal of Business Venturing*, *27*(4), 414–435. doi:10.1016/j.jbusvent.2011.11.006

Luthans, F., & Youssef-Morgan, C. M. (2017). Psychological capital: An evidence-based positive approach. *Annual Review of Organizational Psychology and Organizational Behavior*, *4*(1), 339–366. doi:10.1146/annurev-orgpsych-032516-113324

Lu, C., Wang, H., Lu, J., Du, D., & Bakker, A. B. (2014). Does work engagement increase person-job fit? The role of job crafting and job insecurity. *Journal of Vocational Behavior*, *84*(2), 142–152. doi:10.1016/j.jvb.2013.12.004

Maslach, C., Schaufeli, W. B., & Leiter, M. P. (2001). Job burnout. *Annual Review of Psychology*, *52*, 397–422. doi:10.1146/annurev.psych.52.1.397

Matz, S. C., Kosinski, M., Nave, G., & Stillwell, D. J. (2017). Psychological targeting as an effective approach to digital mass persuasion. *Proceedings of the National Academy of Sciences*. 201710966. doi:10.1073/pnas.1710966114

Rindermann, H., & Thompson, J. (2011). Cognitive capitalism: The effect of cognitive ability on wealth, as mediated through scientific achievement and economic freedom. *Psychological Science*, *22*(6), 754–763. doi:10.1177/0956797611407207

Roberge, M. É., & van Dick, R. (2010). Recognizing the benefits of diversity: When and how does diversity increase group performance? *Human Resource Management Review*, *20*(4), 295–308. doi:10.1016/j.hrmr.2009.09.002

Stone, D. L., Deadrick, D. L., Lukaszewski, K. M., & Johnson, R. (2015). The influence of technology on the future of human resource management. *Human Resource Management Review*, *25*(2), 216–231. doi:10.1016/j.hrmr.2015.01.002

Suen, H. Y., Chen, M. Y. C., & Lu, S. H. (2019). Does the use of synchrony and artificial intelligence in video interviews affect interview ratings and applicant attitudes? *Computers in Human Behavior*, *98*(43), 93–101. doi:10.1016/j.chb.2019.04.012

Wille, B., De Fruyt, F., Dingemanse, S. A., & Vergauwe, J. (2015). A closer look at the psychological diversity within Holland interest types: Construct validation of the career insight questionnaire. *Consulting Psychology Journal: Practice and Research*, *67*(3), 234–257. doi:10.1037/cpb0000041

Winsborough, D., & Chamorro-Premuzic, T. (2013). Consulting psychology in the digital era: Current trends and future directions. *Consulting Psychology Journal: Practice and Research*, *65*(4), 319–324. doi:10.1037/a0035698

Yarkoni, T., & Westfall, J. (2017). Choosing prediction over explanation in psychology: Lessons from machine learning. *Perspectives on Psychological Science*, *12*(6), 1100–1122. doi:10.1177/1745691617693393

2

TALENT AND THE DATA SCIENCE REVOLUTION

It is an understatement to say that we are living in a data revolution. The only way to have stayed "off the grid" for the last 20 years is if you lived on a deserted island. Nearly every aspect of our lives is now shaped by digital technology. From the moment we wake up to the moment we go to sleep, we are interfacing with a black slab of internet connected glass, be it our phones, laptops, or watches. You may even fall into the 27% of Americans who let Jeff Bezos listen in to your household conversations via its Alexa devices (Perez, 2019). These advances in technology have fundamentally changed the way we communicate, consume, and work. To psychologists like us, what is most remarkable about these developments is that behavior which is mediated by digital technology is behavior that is empirically coded and ready to be analyzed by artificially intelligent algorithms that can understand complex patterns and make predictions about our thoughts, desires, and preferences. If the separation between our offline and online self is now non-existent, how is the world of talent identification and recruitment changing?

In this chapter, we explore how the data revolution is changing the science and practice of talent. We will start by outlining how we perceive the current state of the talent landscape and the limitations associated existing approaches to talent identification. We will then describe how the explosion of data and AI is forging new opportunities to mine a multitude of "talent signals" and drastically improve the way we measure and predict one's potential to perform. Finally, we provide recommendations for practitioners looking to not only stay ahead of this fast-moving space, but also advice on how to evaluate the accuracy and ethics of these tools and ensure that they are used responsibly and to their fullest within their organizations.

At the end of this chapter, you will be able to answer the following questions:

1. What are key challenges facing the talent economy and are current tools fit for purpose?

2. What does talent look like in the age of AI?

3. How is the data revolution changing the science of talent?

4. How can I evaluate the accuracy and suitability of new assessment technologies?

5. How can I ensure my HR team uses these new tools in an ethical and effective way?

THE WAR FOR OR ON TALENT?

More than 20 years have passed since McKinsey described the "war for talent" – the idea being that attracting and retaining the very best employees would become an organizational resource that is as important as intellectual property, products, and market dominance (Michaels & Handfield-Jones, 2017). Since then, organizations have invested heavily into improving its hiring practices. So much so that HR has mostly bifurcated letting automation technology take care of the administrative tasks such as compensation and benefits, while staffing talent management divisions whose sole purpose is to create practices that recruit the very best talent, keep them engaged and ensure the organization has healthy pipeline of leaders to execute strategic goals. Like any war, its soldiers need the latest weaponry. Unfortunately, this is not the case for most HR departments.

Despite the enthusiasm and recognition of talent being a key differentiator, most organizations have continued to build its talent practices around outdated, unscientific, and ineffective tools. If you study the results of yearly employee surveys produced by firms such as Gallup, you'll see that the war for talent was never resolved. Many of the top organizations such as Google and Microsoft still struggle to fill pivotal roles – despite the average adult being smarter than previous generations and having greater access to online education resources (Trahan, Stuebing, Fletcher, & Hiscock, 2014). If the biggest and most influential organizations are struggling to recruit and retain the best talent, the picture is likely much worse for smaller business.

One could even argue that the war *for* talent has in fact turned into the war *on* talent. For example, surveys that track employee engagement levels around the world have consistently reported that as much as 87% of the global workforce is not engaged (Mann & Harter, 2016). These data suggest rather than organizations nurturing talent and placing individuals into roles that suit their skills and interests, they have instead created cultures that lead many to feel unsatisfied and frustrated, leaving their talents underutilized and wasted. The inability to place the right people in the roles not only costs organizations serious dollars in unrealized performance (Sorenson & Garman, 2013) but disengagement and poor management breeds counterproductive work behaviors, such as bullying, harassment, theft, and corporate fraud (Chen, Richard, Dorian Boncoeur, & Ford, 2020; Kim, Kolb, & Kim, 2013).

When it comes to selecting and developing leaders, the situation is much worse. It is estimated that around 30% of the variability in team- and organization-level engagement can be attributed to the leader, which suggests that even the most successful organizations are experiencing leadership problems (Kim et al., 2013). Academic reviews estimate that the baseline for leadership failure is around 50% (Hogan, Curphy, & Hogan, 1994), and opinion polls report a strong negative correlation between the amount of money spent on leadership selection and development interventions, and people's confidence in their leaders (Kaiser & Curphy, 2013). One only has to search "my boss is" or "my manager is" to get a sense of the typical experience employees have of their bosses. As the saying goes, people join companies but quit their bosses.

Rising disengagement and toxic bosses not only results in performance losses, but further compounds an organization's struggle to execute its strategy as top talent leaves to join the competition or traditional employment altogether (Rastogi, Pati, Krishnan, & Krishnan, 2018). With 28% of US adults now self-employed (a number that has been steadily increasing; Intuit Quickbooks, 2019) and a further 70% estimated to be considering self-employment (Miller, 2021), many are increasingly trading in their steady salary, security, and benefits for a career that is more fulfilling and autonomous – despite the high chance of failure, lower pay, and longer hours (Intuit Quickbooks, 2019). These trends have been accelerated by the gig economy where tech platforms make it easier for individuals to freelance and apply their expertise. It is now estimated that 36% of the US working population receive either their full or partial salary through gig economy apps such as Uber, Fiverr, or Upwork (Gallup, 2018). Fed up, frustrated, and free from traditional forms of employment, people have more options when it comes to their careers, and organizations are often ill equipped to provide compelling reasons to join them.

The Covid-19 is also drastically changing the nature of work. The pandemic has accelerated business and techno-logical trends that have been developing over the last decade. For example, many organizations who had been pursuing "digital transformation" for years were forced to move to Zoom and DropBox overnight. Similarly, the benefits of coworking spaces and "digital nomadism" that have chal-lenged long held notions of what work looks like, and where we do it, are looking increasingly more convincing. Forced to work from home during lockdown many had the opportunity to experience new ways of working, and at the time of writing, it is estimated that 60% of people want to continue working remotely and are uninterested in returning to their physical offices (Strouther, 2020).

Pre-pandemic, the virtues of remote over in-person ways of working were hotly debated. Yet a year later, we can now recognize that people can be trusted to work hard, produc-tivity doesn't slump when people are given the freedom to choose where they work, and that there are significant improvements to work-life balance (Spiggle, 2020). Under-standably, many miss the in-person interactions with their colleagues that help them feel connected, boost creativity, and provide a sense of belonging (Methot, Gabriel, Downes, & Rosado-Solomon, 2021). To align these shifting attitudes with organizational priorities, many leaders are now faced with the difficulty of designing hybrid workplaces that provide its employees with flexibility to choose how, when, and where they work. This new type of workplace poses fresh challenges for talent management. First, how do you create work practices that accommodate those who wish to stay remote versus those who want to be in an office? Second, are your hiring practices sophisticated enough to identify and onboard virtual talent? Last, how do you plan to reward, promote, and develop talent when not located in the same office?

Given these challenges, it is easy to be optimistic about the future of the talent economy, because in some ways it is hard for things to get worse. Let's be clear, the blame for these poor talent practices is shared by many. A portion of the blame can be directed to overconfident talent leaders who value intuition over data, another portion at the vendors who push bullshit tools or have artificially inflated the cost and complexity of scientific tools so that they are not used beyond the C-Suite, and another portion at I-O psychologists who have done a terrible job at translating the science into practice.

While the data revolution will bring change and the opportunity to do things better, the good news is that the essence of talent is unlikely to change. This means that we can continue to leverage and apply over 100 years of scientific research on what makes someone talented. In line with Chamorro-Premuzic, Akhtar, Winsborough, and Sherman (2017), we argue that talent will always be understood in terms of four basic heuristics, namely:

- *The rule of the vital few:* As illustrated by Pareto's principle, in any group or collective of individuals, a relatively small proportion of members will account for a disproportion-ately large amount of group output or performance. These "vital few" may be considered an organization's "top talent."

- *The maximal performance rule:* There is a well-known premise within I-O Psychology that stipulates that the best way to test a person's ability is by evaluating the best they *can do*. Regardless of the talent domain, this so-called *maximal performance* rule will always be useful to identify systematic individual differences in talent or competence. Importantly, people must want to do their best in order to display their talents, so there is no reason to expect individuals to perform to the best of their capabilities at all points in time (Sackett, 2007).

- *The effortless performance rule:* Another classic I-O tenet essentially defines performance as talent + effort. Simple algebra then suggests that, talent = performance–effort. In other words, talented people will generally require less effort to achieve a certain level of performance than their less talented counterparts will. In other words, when individuals exert the same level of effort, performance differences between them will remain, unless they have the exact same level of talent. By the same token, early manifestations of talent, such as precocious talent, stand out because of their effortless performance: for example, Messi in football, Mozart in music, and Marie Curie in science. With limited training and practice, they are able to surpass more seasoned and experienced, but less talented, counterparts.

- *Personality in the right place:* A final heuristic that will remain in place for understanding talent in the future is that talent emerges from personality being in the right place. That is, when there is a strong match between people's default predispositions and the characteristics of their respective jobs or roles, their talent emerges as result, which fuels future career development. In line with this idea, all talent management interventions can ultimately be seen as an attempt to enhance person-job fit, and in turn job performance.

It is important to acknowledge that despite the rapidly changing circumstances of work, the essential ingredients of talent are unlikely to change any time soon, at least when it comes to human talent. Thus in any domain of competence or expertise, an individual's probability to be designated as "talented" will increase if they are more able, socially skilled, and driven (Hogan, Chamorro-Premuzic, & Kaiser, 2013). Ability includes both general intelligence and domain-specific expertise, encompassing what a person can learn and has learned. Social skills concern empathy, intra- and interpersonal competence, and likability. Drive concerns ambition and conscientiousness, which can accelerate or inhibit any degree of talent. In an age when organizations devote an enormous amount of time to creating their own extensive competency models, often to reinvent the wheel or introduce an unnecessary level of complexity, hiring managers would be well advised to remain focused on these general ingredients of talent in order to identify their most valuable employees. When it comes to the future of talent selection, the *how* will change but the *what* will not.

HOW EFFECTIVE ARE CURRENT PRACTICES?

Science and practice rarely move in tandem, with one often lagging behind the other. This is most true when it comes to identifying and recruiting talent. While some organizations have an appetite for evidence-based selection practices, a trend that is growing, many still rely on methodologies that have been demonstrated to have low empirical reliability and validity (Chamorro-Premuzic, 2017). That is, they lack the ability to accurately or consistently measure one's talents and predict their ability to perform on the job. Fortunately, using theory and data, a great deal is now known about how to identify those individuals who have the potential to perform and create value for their organizations.

To understand where recruitment is going, it is important to understand where it has been and where we currently are. In this section, we review three popular practices, highlighting their strengths and limitations.

Interviews

It seems almost inconceivable that any form of selection task and decision is not informed by one, indeed many, job interviews. In fact, it is estimated that 90% of employment selection decisions involve interviews (Cook, 2016) and have been used in selection for over two centuries (e.g. the Royal Navy used job interviews as early as 1800). Whether it comes at the beginning or the end of the selection process, the selection interview is thought to be a crucial and central part of the process, whereby the employer and applicant can help achieve a mutual understanding of one another and make inferences about the suitability of the applicant. Of all the selection methods, they are rated as the most acceptable method. Given their ubiquity, are interviews sufficient to identify talented employees?

A seminal meta-analysis by Cook (2016) investigated the how accurate interviews were in predicting job performance. Aggregating results from over 500 scientific studies, Cook found that the validity coefficient for interviews as predictors of job performance is $r = 0.15$. While the validity for structured interviews was higher ($r = 0.28$), most employment interviews are unstructured (Chauhan, 2019). These results suggest that at best the employment interview explains a paltry 5%–6% of the variance in future job performance.

Aside from their low predictive validity, there are two other important issues associated with interviews. First, they are costly and demand a significant amount of time from both the interviewer and the candidate. This creates issues when trying to identify talent at volume. Therefore, interviews are unlikely to deliver a return on investment when compared to the cost, delivery, and validity of other tools. Second, the interview process and the subsequent decision might be influenced by implicit cognitive biases and heuristics. Implicit biases and heuristics shape the way interviewers process information, make decisions, and form judgments of others. The use of heuristics and biases increases as our cognitive load increases – a state that is commonplace for the overworked and busy hiring manager. Biases and heuristic are natural and experienced by everyone, however they can at best lead to poor and irrational decisions and at worst, prejudiced, and discriminatory evaluations. For example, implicit heuristics can explain why minority groups are adversely selected in job interviews (Purkiss, Perrewé, Gillespie, Mayes, & Ferris, 2006).

Biodata

Biodata measures have informed selection decisions for many years and are still widely used in certain areas of employment, such as sales and insurance. In broad terms, biodata measures include information about a person's background and life history (e.g. civil status, previous education, and employment), ranging from objectively determined dates – date of first job, time in last job, years of higher education – to subjective preferences, such as those encompassed by personality traits. Biodata are most commonly collected through resumes and job application forms.

The main assumption underlying the use of biodata is that the "best predictor of future performance is past performance" (Wernimont & Campbell, 1968), though biodata focus as much on the *predictors* of past performance as on past performance itself. Indeed, it has been argued that one of the greatest potential routes for understanding and improving the prediction of work performance is the relationship between individuals' life history and their performance at work (Fleishman, 1988), a question directly related to biodata. Is there evidence to support this assumption?

A meta-analysis by (Bliesener, 1996) involving over 100 samples found that, when correcting for methodological artifacts and statistical errors, the overall validity for biodata inventories was $r = 0.22$. Bliesener concluded that

> *Biographical data are a valid predictor of an applicant's suitability. This, combined with their high economy, their universal applicability and the ease of combining them with other predictive procedures, makes them a valuable instrument in personnel selection.*

> (1996, p. 118)

Given that biodata measures are able to exceed the validity and limitations of interviews, what are its drawbacks?

First, for biodata to be a valid, they must be first scored correctly. In practice, this is often not the case, such as when resumes and application forms are judged subjectively as a check for basic requirements and to inform an interview discussion. Applying a sound scoring methodology is preferred to human judgments that are subject to the aforementioned biases, heuristics, idiosyncrasies, and inconsistencies.

Secondly, biodata are prone to faking as recruiters rarely invest the time to follow up with references and do appropriate investigative work because of time restrictions. Similarly, research has shown that when comparing biodata between applicants and incumbents, and when scored correctly, the former have inflated scores (Harold, McFarland, & Weekley, 2006). This demonstrates that just like interviews, biodata measures are susceptible to impression management and faking-good.

Psychometric Assessments

The scientific study of individual differences adopts a perspective whereby dispositions in thought, feelings, and behavior are continuous, roughly normally distributed, and can be accurately measured through data-driven practices called psychometrics. Psychometric assessments are survey-like tools that seek to measure relevant psychological constructs. Not only do they overcome the limitations of both interviews and biodata; psychometrically developed assessments have the potential to offer superior predictive validity. Two psychological constructs that have received the most attention and practical use are personality and cognitive ability.

There are many models and taxonomies of personality (i.e. temporally and situationally stable behavioral tendencies and characteristics), yet the most influential and empirically supported framework is the "Five Factor Model" (McCrae & Costa, 1987). According to this model, personality can be organized around five broad, distinct, and continuous dimensions: openness, conscientiousness, extroversion, agreeableness, and emotional stability. Each of the five dimensions has been found to predict critical work outcomes. For example, conscientiousness and job performance ($r = 0.22$; Barrick & Mount, 1991), extraversion and leadership effectiveness ($r = 0.19$;

Bono & Judge, 2004), openness and innovation ($r = 0.49$; Batey, Chamorro-Premuzic, & Furnham, 2010), agreeableness and organizational citizenship ($r = 0.36$; Ilies, Scott, & Judge, 2006), and emotional stability and job burnout ($r = 0.36$; Bakker, Van Der Zee, Lewig, & Dollard, 2006).

Intelligence describes the extent to which people can solve complex problems, understand abstract patterns, and engage in critical thought (Chamorro-Premuzic & Furnham, 2010). Of all the psychological constructs and tools to identify talent, intelligence remains the single most predictive construct of positive work outcomes. A meta-analysis by Hunter and Hunter (1984) found that intelligence consistently predicted job performance across multiple levels of job complexity, with validity coefficients ranging between 0.23 and 0.58. Similarly, another meta-analysis by Bertua, Anderson, and Salgado (2005) found intelligence to predict job and training performance ($r = 0.48$; $r = 0.50$). In fact, when intelligence tests are combined with other selection tools such as interviews or personality assessment, the predictive validity can increase to over 0.60, which is likely near the ceiling of the predictive power of selection tests.

Despite their evidence in support of predictive validity, psychometric assessments are not without their limitations. First, they can be cumbersome and lengthy to complete, resulting in a poor user experience. Second, they may lack face validity and therefore be treated with suspicion by the test taker. Third, they rely on self-assessment and therefore raising concerns around faking-good. Although this is not an issue with intelligence tests, as there is a right or wrong answer, this final point has created much debate within the field given mixed evidence that faking does or does not harm their utility and validity (Schmitt, 2014). Finally, well-designed psychometric assessments have traditionally been costly, meaning that they are most used at senior levels. Fortunately, the next generation of assessments are quickly providing solutions to these limitations.

TALENT ASSESSMENT IN THE AGE OF AI

As discussed in the previous section, the assessment process has largely remained unchanged in the last 50 years. We still rely on cumbersome and inaccurate methods such as the interview or CV, while the only innovation to happen to scientific tools like psychometric assessments is to go from paper and pencil to online. These methodologies are limited not only due to their inability to scale and lack of sophistication, but also because they have simply not kept up with the changing nature of work and how people are living their lives. Given that the foundational premise of selection practices is to make predictions about how one will behave in the future, the age of AI creates an exciting opportunity to improve current assessment practices by incorporating large amounts of diverse and objective data points about individuals and build highly accurate profiles to shape hiring decisions in seconds.

AI-powered talent algorithms use more than traditional talent indictors. Instead, they can take advantage of the millions of digital records we generate each day. It is now estimated that the average person now produces over 146,880 megabytes of data a day, a number that continues to increase each year as we deeply integrate digital devices and services into our lives (Andre, 2021). Meanwhile our sensor-packed devices are continuously capturing digital records of the decisions we make, the content we consume, and the people we interact with. Together these two sources of data provide all of the input needed to bring about a new era of talent assessment.

As the saying goes, "the future is already here, it just not evenly distributed" (Gibson, 2003). This is true for the use of novel data sources and methods in the recruitment space. For example, while we may feel squeamish about recruiters using social media to *snoop* or *research* candidates (it depends on what side of the process you're on), it is a practice that has already become deeply embedded into the hiring process. It is estimated that 84% of firms use social media sites for recruitment; 44% use candidate social media profiles to screen candidates; and 36% have disqualified candidates on the basis of information found (Society for Human Resource Management, 2017). To place these figures in context, the use of social media evaluations in hiring decisions is more prevalent than traditional methods such as psychometric inventories (20%), and as popular as aptitude tests (42%; Davison, Bing, Kluemper, & Roth, 2016; Rogelberg, 2006). Having public and easily searchable information about candidates is clearly of value to recruiters, however, scientific studies demonstrate human evaluations of social media are fraught with the same in-group and out-group biases that plague interviews and other types of talent judgements (not to mention the obvious ethical concerns around privacy and consent; Jeske & Shultz, 2016). Fortunately, the data revolution and the use of AI can overcome these in four ways:

- Digital platforms and devices can objectively measure behavior, removing the need for biased human evaluations (Javed & Brishti, 2020).

- AI algorithms can be optimized to maximize the prediction between our digital records and performance indictors (Javed & Brishti, 2020).

- AI's ability to scale and thereby reach a greater number of candidates from different backgrounds, can create more diverse and more efficient hiring pipelines (Javed & Brishti, 2020).

- AI algorithms can provide greater transparency into how data are used and weighted to reach a hiring decision, thereby producing fairer and more ethical practices (Javed & Brishti, 2020).

The underlying premise that I-O psychologists use to justify and explain the use of digital records and AI in the future of recruitment is the "theory of talent signals" (Chamorro-Premuzic, Winsborough, Sherman, & Hogan, 2016). First inspired by psychological research that has found our personality, values, and demographics to be accurately inferred by the way we decorate our homes (Fingerman, Kim, Zhang, Ng, & Birditt, 2021; Gosling, Ko, Mannarelli, & Morris, 2002), the things we buy (Kassarjian, 1971; Sandy, Gosling, & Durant, 2013), media we consume (Kraaykamp, 2001), and physical locations we frequent (Kim & Song, 2014), the theory of talent signals extend this research into the realm of online behavior. Specifically, as we live out our lives through online platforms and devices, we leave active (i.e. text posts, purchases, photos, videos, etc.) or passive (i.e. metadata, browser history, endorsements and "likes," etc.) records of our behavior. While each record of behavior may not reveal much, when aggregated across many sources of input and points in time, AI has the ability to mine these records for unique patterns of behavior to reveal what makes you, you (Siege, 2015). The very nature of AI means that if digital records are incorporated into the assessment and selection experience, we can move away from delivering expensive and hands-on processes that rarely produce helpful insights, to an automated and near-instant practice that produces data-driven recommendations that surpass human evaluations.

These ideas are not hypothetical, they continue to be proved out by a growing number of startups offering novel assessment products and an interdisciplinary body of scientific research that shows talent signals can not only be identified through 'big data,' but AI can make meaningful predictions from these data about future behavior. Exploring this research and its applications is the focus of subsequent chapters, however it is important to highlight the work of Dr. Michal Kosinki and Dr. David Stillwell, whose team were the first to kickstart this area of academic research and spawn this emerging industry.

In a series of studies, this team showed that a computer algorithm could be trained to interpret the pattern of "likes" on Facebook and produce accurate classifications of users' personality, gender, voting preferences, and even sexual orientation (Kosinski, 2013; Kosinski, Stillwell, & Graepel, 2013; Lambiotte & Kosinski, 2014; Schwartz et al., 2013). Others have replicated this work, extending the findings to relationships between the images people post, their language, and even dark side personality traits – unconscious traits which negatively affect performance at work and interpersonal relationships (Akhtar, Winsborough, Ort, Johnson, & Chamorro-Premuzic, 2018; Liu, Preoţiuc-Pietro, Samani, Moghaddam, & Ungar, 2016; Ortigosa, Carro, & Quiroga, 2014). Chapters 3–5 will unpack these methodologies to reveal how AI can process web behavior, biometrics, and even video game behavior to predict key markers of talent and performance.

The data revolution is also reshaping internal talent decision-making through the next generation of People Analytics. Using data to understand and improve the employee lifecycle has become a common practice for many large organizations. As much of the modern work experience is conducted through Zoom, Slack, and other collaboration tools (and increasingly so thanks to Covid-19), employee's digital footprints can be mined to better understand their engagement (Gelbard, Ramon-Gonen, Carmeli, Bittmann, & Talyansky, 2018), how they collaborate with others (Gelbard et al., 2018), performance and intention to live (Gelbard et al., 2018), counterproductive work behaviors (Gelbard et al., 2018), and the company culture (Gelbard et al., 2018). Having access to these insights in real-time and across the entire organization could go a long way to solve many of the issues outlined at the start of this chapter, thus building better employees, teams, and leaders.

When it comes to making people decisions using AI algorithms, there are two common reactions. The first is to outright deny that AI algorithms are better judges of talent than people (scientific studies suggest that just isn't true; Kuncel, Klieger, Connelly, & Ones, 2013). The second is the knee-jerk reaction that the use of AI in decision-making is a zero-sum game whereby decisions can only be made by a human or a computer. While AI is increasingly automating and unconsciously nudging the way we live our lives (see your Netflix or Spotify recommendations), and it's easy to find examples of poor or lazy implementation of AI tools that go haywire (see Microsoft's racist chatbot, Tay; Schwartz, 2019), the recommendations of experts in this field call for integrated processes (Kochan, 2018). Specifically, hiring managers should view AI algorithms as a helpful new colleague, that will enhance and not replace their knowledge and expertise (Li, Lassiter, & Lee, 2021). Humans are terrible judges of talent, yet evidence shows that we can counter our biases and limitations when given objective insights whose margins of error can be calculated and understood (Li et al., 2021). Put differently, the next CEO of Amazon will be not selected by an algorithm, but we can be certain that AI will produce a set of insights to be considered alongside the evaluations of the company's Board. Until we can produce *generalized artificial intelligence*, the future of talent assessment will be integrated between human and machine, balancing each other's limitations while complementing their strengths.

UNDERSTANDING THE EFFECTIVENESS OF NEW TOOLS

So far we have explored all of the benefits that the future of assessment will bring – faster, more accurate, cheaper – but it is important to understand their limitations, trade-offs, and what is needed to build high-performing and ethical AI talent algorithms. This is helpful to not only counter the hype and bullshit marketing that is in this space (sadly there is no shortage), but also helps us recognize what type of novel assessment solution should be used when, where, and how.

To help you evaluate the suitability and effectiveness of new talent assessments (and much of what we present throughout this book), there a few concepts you must consider. First, what are algorithms and how they are developed. Second, what does it mean for an assessment to be *reliable* and *valid*. Last, to acknowledge the potential for bias and know how to mitigate it.

Algorithms are simply a set of rules or instructions for a computer to follow and produce calculations or estimates about one's probability to behave in a certain way or belong to a group. For example, an algorithm could be developed to make predictions about one's ability to perform in a role based on their work experience and past performance. Digital records of behavior and AI allow these algorithms to become incredibly complex, leverage vast amounts of data, and become adaptive – that is the algorithm continues to tune and improve itself.

Algorithms are usually developed by first collecting a dataset from a large representative sample. This dataset contains *predictors* variables and *outcomes* variables. Within the context of HR, the predictors are usually attributes about one's career experience, psychological profile, or previous behavior, while the outcome variables are the desired states that you would like to know about someone's potential (i.e. ability to perform on the job, leadership effectiveness, retention, etc.). Once the data have been collected, the computer is instructed to spot and detect patterns between these two sets of variables, and produce a set of instructions that can be used to make inferences about others' potential. For discussion on how to develop and implement your own algorithms, see Chamorro-Premuzic, Polli, & Dattner, 2019; Kulkarni & Che, 2019; Mujtaba & Mahapatra, 2019.

To evaluate the quality of any assessment, be it traditional or algorithmic, it is important to understand the assessments' *reliability* and *validity*. These terms are important psychometric concepts that are used throughout the industry and provide helpful information for practitioners looking for information to know what assessment tools actually work. Reliability describes the extent to which an assessment measures a particular characteristic or talent consistently. That is, if a candidate is assessed using the same tool across two points in time, they should expect to receive the same result. Working with reliable assessments is important because if one's estimation of talent various each time they complete the assessment, you can never be sure what you are measuring nor have the confidence to form a firm selection decision. Validity describes the extent to which an assessment actually predicts a desired outcome or expected behavior. To evaluate the validity of an assessment we can estimate the correlation between scores on the assessment and the outcome. If there is no correlation, the assessment can be said to have no validity and should not be used in selection processes because it can accurately predict future behavior. Knowing the reliability and validity estimates of novel assessment methods enables us to effectively compare and contrast their accuracy and utility with existing tools.

Finally, to build fair and responsible algorithms and novel assessments, it is important to test their potential for group bias, otherwise known as *adverse impact*. Adverse impact describes how a tool may disparately assess minority groups and thus restrict their ability to fair and equal access to employment opportunities. Adverse impact is coded into US employment law and important issue for many assessment developers (Equal Employment Opportunity Commission, 1978). When it comes to detecting bias in novel assessments, the issue is complicated. Using AI to mine millions of digital records can create a "black box" whereby we lack transparency into what the algorithms are using to build their predictions. Unfortunately, there are examples whereby black box algorithms have created racist and sexist hiring tools (Dastin, 2018). The good news is that as society grows more aware of algorithms' ability to become "weapons of math destruction," there are now many efforts and advancements being made so that AI decision-making is more transparent (HireVue, 2021; Zielinski, 2020). Furthermore, the use of data-driven assessments can allow practitioners to spot and detect bias in a variety of ways that we cannot do with human evaluations. Although it may be uncomfortable to admit, we are unlikely to ever be able to truly rid humans from inherent bias, nor fully understand how we arrive at our decisions. However, using AI-powered tools allows us to control for this and adopt a harm reduction approach to curtail human bias as they can be inspected to reveal how variables are weighted, allowing for further tuning and adjustment. Nonetheless, all assessments (new or old) must be tested using statistical estimations of group differences (i.e. does one group score significantly higher or low than other) and the "4/5ths rule" (i.e. comparing selection rates of minority groups compared to majority groups; Equal Employment Opportunity Commission, 1978). You can jump to Chapter six where we explore the ethical considerations and trade-offs associated with the AI-enabled talent assessments.

PREPARING FOR ALGORITHMIC HR

To harness the opportunity that the data revolution presents, it's clear that HR needs to drastically change the way it operates and how it trains its own practitioners. It is easy to see that the future of HR will be algorithmic – automated workflows will take care of the everyday and traditional tasks while data and AI will become a central tool in talent decision-making (Chamorro-Premuzic et al., 2016). If the war for talent is to still be believed, HR leaders need to begin the work of upskilling their teams otherwise they run the risk of understaffing their organizations and losing talent to competitors. Fortunately, if you are reading this book, you already making proactive attempts to get ahead of this curve. That said, there are three competencies all HR practitioners need to become more comfortable with if they are to implement the emerging technologies we discuss in this book and whatever the future may bring.

Tracking Performance and Business Impact

In our careers, we often meet excited and enthusiastic talent leaders who come to us with the ambition of using AI to predict talent and performance. Unfortunately, this enthusiasm is often not met with the implementation of basic performance management practices. This means that they do not know how to define talent or performance, nor have they operationalized these definitions into objective and high-quality measures of performance. As explained above, to train reliable and valid talent algorithms, data scientists need outcome data to point their predictors at. Without this, the promise of AI cannot be realized.

If AI is to become a valuable tool for hiring managers, it is important that HR leaders spend the time investing in improving their organization's ability to collect accurate performance metrics and more closely attribute job output to individuals. The precision of new tools to predict behavior will be limited by the precision to measure the performance and contributions of individuals. Overcoming this challenge will help leaders demonstrate the ROI and effectiveness of assessment practices and wider talent management strategies.

Data Literacy

Just as HR has increasingly grown to incorporate more I-O psychologists, the future of HR will grow to include technologists and data scientists. This will require HR practitioners becoming *data literate*. That is the ability to interpret data and reach valid conclusions using statistical techniques (Twidale, Blake, & Gant, 2013). The data literate practitioner is able to turn data into the insights and knowledge needed to affect organization change and improve decision-making. While there are encouraging signs that the field of HR is moving in this direction (Launchpad, 2020), practitioners need to learn new hard skills so that they do not become a bottleneck to the use and availability of rich talent signals. We are not calling for HR practitioners to become data scientists, rather than they should acquire a foundation in statistics or data visualization so they can use data to improve decision-making and communicate business requirements to data scientists.

Algorithmic Responsibility

The influential thinker Cathy O'Neil describes how algorithms that are opaque, highly consequential to one's life, and used at scale, as "weapons of math destruction" (O'Neil, 2016). To disarm these "WMDs," HR practitioners need to not only develop expertise in the collection and interpretation of data but become mindful of how algorithms are used and deployed. This requires new skills that allow practitioners to select the right providers and vendors, critically evaluate the effectiveness and limitations of assessment algorithms, and know what safeguards are put in place to detect and remove bias. Being able to explain what data the algorithm uses, how it was developed, the representativeness of the training dataset, and the potential of harmful or untended consequences, is critical for considered and responsible use of algorithms (Dignum, 2019). As algorithms are becoming further intertwined into hiring practices, we expect the HR department of the future to employ a "head of AI ethics" to safeguard against these risks.

The data revolution is here to stay. While the war for talent has been unsuccessful, it is certainly not lost. Each of us produce thousands of talent signals every day, revealing something unique about our personality, talent, and experiences. HR leaders are in a unique position to harness this innovation and transform the way they select and recruit talent. The key challenge for leaders is to start building the in-house expertise that is needed to use these tools to their full potential. Similarly, researchers and technologists must continue their efforts to prove out not only the validity of these new tools, but also demonstrate that they are fairer and more rewarding than the current alternatives.

REFERENCES

Akhtar, R., Winsborough, D., Ort, U., Johnson, A., & Chamorro-Premuzic, T. (2018). Detecting the dark side of personality using social media status updates. *Personality and Individual Differences*, *132*, 90–97. doi:10.1016/J.PAID.2018.05.026

Andre, L. (2021). 53 important statistics about how much data is created every day. Retrieved from https://financesonline.com/how-much-data-is-created-every-day/

Bakker, A. B., Van Der Zee, K. I., Lewig, K. A., & Dollard, M. F. (2006). The relationship between the big five personality factors and burnout: A study among volunteer counselors. *The Journal of Social Psychology*, *146*(1), 31–50. doi:10.3200/SOCP.146.1.31-50

Barrick, M. R., & Mount, M. K. (1991). The Big Five personality dimensions and job performance: A meta-analysis. *Personnel Psychology*, *44*(1), 1–26. doi:10.1111/j.1744-6570.1991.tb00688.x

Batey, M., Chamorro-Premuzic, T., & Furnham, A. (2010). Individual differences in ideational behavior: Can the big five and psychometric intelligence predict creativity scores? *Creativity Research Journal*, *22*(1), 90–97. doi:10.1080/10400410903579627

Bertua, C., Anderson, N., & Salgado, J. F. (2005). The predictive validity of cognitive ability tests: A UK meta-analysis.

Journal of Occupational and Organizational Psychology, 78(3), 387–409. doi:10.1348/096317905X26994

Bliesener, T. (1996). Methodological moderators in validating biographical data in personnel selection. *Journal of Occupational and Organizational Psychology*, 69(1), 107–120. doi:10.1111/j.2044-8325.1996.tb00603.x

Bono, J. E., & Judge, T. A. (2004). Personality and transformational and transactional leadership: A meta-analysis. *Journal of Applied Psychology*, 89(5), 901–910. doi:10.1037/0021-9010.89.5.901

Chamorro-Premuzic, T. (2017). The talent delusion: Why data, not intuition, is the key to unlocking human potential. *Piatkus*.

Chamorro-Premuzic, T., Akhtar, R., Winsborough, D., & Sherman, R. A. (2017). The datafication of talent: How technology is advancing the science of human potential at work. *Current Opinion in Behavioral Sciences*, 18, 13–16. doi:10.1016/j.cobeha.2017.04.007

Chamorro-Premuzic, T., & Furnham, A. (2010). *The psychology of personnel selection*. Cambridge: Cambridge University Press. doi:10.1037/h0052197

Chamorro-Premuzic, T., Polli, F., & Dattner, B. (2019). Building ethical AI for talent management. *Harvard Business Review*. Digital Articles, 2–5. Retrieved from https://hbr.org/2019/11/building-ethical-ai-for-talent-management

Chamorro-Premuzic, T., Winsborough, D., Sherman, R. A., & Hogan, R. (2016). New talent signals: Shiny new objects or a brave new world? *Industrial and Organizational Psychology*, 9(3), 621–640. doi:10.1017/iop.2016.6

Chauhan, R. S. (2019). Unstructured interviews: Are they really all that bad? *Human Resource Development International*, 1–14. doi:10.1080/13678868.2019.1603019

Chen, H., Richard, O. C., Dorian Boncoeur, O., & Ford, D. L. (2020). Work engagement, emotional exhaustion, and counterproductive work behavior. *Journal of Business Research*, *114*, 30–41. doi:10.1016/J.JBUSRES.2020.03.025

Cook, M. (2016). *Personnel selection: Adding value through people-A changing picture*. Hoboken, NJ: John Wiley & Sons.

Dastin, J. (2018). Amazon scraps secret AI recruiting tool that showed bias against women. Retrieved from https://www.reuters.com/article/us-amazon-com-jobs-automation-insight-idUSKCN1MK08G

Davison, K. K., Bing, M. N., Kluemper, D. H., & Roth, P. L. (2016). Social media as a personnel selection and hiring resource: Reservations and recommendations. In *Social media in employee selection and recruitment: Theory, practice, and current challenges* (pp. 15–42). doi:10.1007/978-3-319-29989-1_2

Dignum, V. (2019). *Responsible artificial intelligence: How to develop and use AI in a responsible way*. New York, NY: Springer.

Equal Employment Opportunity Commission. (1978). Uniform guidelines on employee selection procedures. *Federal Register*, *43*(166), 38290–38315.

Fingerman, K. L., Kim, Y. K., Zhang, S., Ng, Y. T., & Birditt, K. S. (2021). Late life in the living room: Room décor, functional limitations, and personality. *The Gerontologist*. doi:10.1093/geront/gnab093

Fleishman, E. A. (1988). Some new frontiers in personnel selection research. *Personnel Psychology*, *41*(4), 679–701. doi:10.1111/j.1744-6570.1988.tb00647.x

Gallup. (2018). The gig economy and alternative work arrangements. Retrieved from https://www.gallup.com/workplace/240878/gig-economy-paper-2018.aspx

Gelbard, R., Ramon-Gonen, R., Carmeli, A., Bittmann, R. M., & Talyansky, R. (2018). Sentiment analysis in organizational work: Towards an ontology of people analytics. *Expert Systems*, *35*(5), e12289. doi:10.1111/EXSY.12289

Gibson, W. (2003, May 3). The future is already here – It's just not evenly distributed. *The Economist*.

Gosling, S. D., Ko, S., Mannarelli, T., & Morris, M. E. (2002). A room with a cue: Personality judgments based on offices and bedrooms. *Journal of Personality and Social Psychology*, *82*(3), 379–398. doi:10.1037/0022-3514.82.3.379

Harold, C. M., McFarland, L. A., & Weekley, J. A. (2006). The validity of verifiable and non-verifiable biodata items: An examination across applicants and incumbents. *International Journal of Selection and Assessment*, *14*(4), 336–346. doi:10.1111/j.1468-2389.2006.00355.x

HireVue. (2021). HireVue leads the industry with commitment to transparent and ethical use of AI in hiring. Retrieved from https://www.hirevue.com/press-release/hirevue-leads-the-industry-with-commitment-to-transparent-and-ethical-use-of-ai-in-hiring

Hogan, R., Chamorro-Premuzic, T., & Kaiser, R. B. (2013). Employability and career success: Bridging the gap between theory and reality. *Industrial and Organizational Psychology*, *6*(1), 3–16. doi:10.1111/iops.12001

Hogan, R., Curphy, G. J., & Hogan, J. (1994). What we know about Leadership: Effectiveness and personality. *American Psychologist*, *49*(6), 493–504. doi:10.1037/0003-066x.49.6.493

Hunter, J. E., & Hunter, R. F. (1984). Validity and utility of alternative predictors of job performance. *Psychological Bulletin*, *96*(1), 72–98. doi:10.1037/0033-2909.96.1.72

Ilies, R., Scott, B. A., & Judge, T. A. (2006). The interactive effects of personal traits and experienced states on intra-individual patterns of citizenship behavior. *Academy of Management Journal*, *49*(3), 561–575. doi:10.5465/AMJ.2006.21794672

Intuit Quickbooks. (2019). *Gig economy and self-employment report*. Mountain View, CA. Retrieved from https://quickbooks.intuit.com/content/dam/intuit/quickbooks/Gig-Economy-Self-Employment-Report-2019.pdf

Javed, A., & Brishti, J. K. (2020). The viability of AI-based recruitment: A systematic literature review. Umea University. Retrieved from https://www.diva-portal.org/smash/get/diva2:1442986/FULLTEXT01.pdf

Jeske, D., & Shultz, K. S. (2016). Using social media content for screening in recruitment and selection: Pros and cons. *Work, Employment & Society*, *30*(3), 535–546. doi:10.1177/0950017015613746

Kaiser, R. B., & Curphy, G. (2013). Leadership development: The failure of an industry and the opportunity for consulting psychologists. *Consulting Psychology Journal*, *65*(4), 294–302. doi:10.1037/a0035460

Kassarjian, H. H. (1971). Personality and consumer behavior: A review. *Journal of Marketing Research*, *8*(4), 409–418. https://www.jstor.org/stable/3150229

Kim, W., Kolb, J. A., & Kim, T. (2013). The relationship between work engagement and performance. *Human Resource Development Review*, *12*(3), 248–276. doi:10. 1177/1534484312461635

Kim, S. Y., & Song, H. Y. (2014). Predicting human location based on human personality. *Lecture Notes in Computer Science*, *8638*, 70–81. doi:10.1007/978-3-319-10353-2_7

Kochan, T. (2018). AI integration—A better approach. Retrieved from https://www.brinknews.com/ai-integration-a-better-approach/

Kosinski, M. (2013). Facebook Likes show big data brings big responsibility. Retrieved from https://www.proquest.com/docview/1317443997?accountid=50247

Kosinski, M., Stillwell, D., & Graepel, T. (2013). Private traits and attributes are predictable from digital records of human behavior. *Proceedings of the National Academy of Sciences*, *110*(15), 5802–5805. doi:10.1073/pnas.1218772110

Kraaykamp, G. (2001). Parents, personality and media preferences. *Communications*, *26*(1), 15–36. doi:10.1515/comm.2001.26.1.15

Kulkarni, S., & Che, X. (2019). Intelligent software tools for recruiting. *Journal of International Technology and Information Management*, *28*(2), 2–16. Retrieved from https://scholarworks.lib.csusb.edu/jitimAvailableat:https://scholarworks.lib.csusb.edu/jitim/vol28/iss2/1

Kuncel, N. R., Klieger, D. M., Connelly, B. S., & Ones, D. S. (2013). Mechanical versus clinical data combination in selection and admissions decisions: A meta-analysis. *Journal of Applied Psychology*, *98*(6), 1060–1072. doi:10. 1037/a0034156

Lambiotte, R., & Kosinski, M. (2014). Tracking the digital footprints of personality. *Proceedings of the IEEE*, *102*(12), 1934–1939. doi:10.1109/JPROC.2014.2359054

Launchpad. (2020). How data is rocking the world of HR and recruitment. Retrieved from https://launchpadrecruits.com/insight-articles/why-data-is-rocking-the-world-of-hr-and-recruitment

Li, L., Lassiter, T., & Lee, M. K. (2021). Algorithmic hiring in practice: Recruiter and HR professional's perspectives on AI use in hiring. In Proceedings of the 2021 AAAI/ACM Conference on AI, Ethics, and Society. doi:10.1145/3461702.3462531

Liu, L., Preoţiuc-Pietro, D., Samani, Z. R., Moghaddam, M. E., & Ungar, L. (2016). Analyzing personality through social media profile picture choice. In Proceedings of the 10th International Conference on Web and Social Media (pp. 211–220). Retrieved from https://www.aaai.org/ocs/index.php/ICWSM/ICWSM16/paper/view/13102

Mann, A., & Harter, J. (2016). The worldwide employee engagement crisis. Retrieved from https://www.gallup.com/workplace/236495/worldwide-employee-engagement-crisis.aspx

McCrae, R. R., & Costa, P. T. (1987). Validation of the five-factor model of personality across instruments and observers. *Journal of Personality and Social Psychology*, *52*(1), 81–90. doi:10.1037/0022-3514.52.1.81

Methot, J. R., Gabriel, A. S., Downes, P., & Rosado-Solomon, E. (2021). Remote workers need small talk, too. Retrieved from https://hbr.org/2021/03/remote-workers-need-small-talk-too

Michaels, E., & Handfield-Jones, H. (2017). The war for talent. *McKinsey Quarterly*, 44–57. https://www.proquest.com/docview/224542898?pq-origsite=gscholar&fromopenview=true

Miller, G. E. (2021). 70% of Americans want to be self-employed. What is stopping you? Retrieved from https://20somethingfinance.com/self-employment-poll/

Mujtaba, D. F., & Mahapatra, N. R. (2019). Ethical considerations in AI-based recruitment. *IEEE International Symposium on Technology and Society*. doi:10.1109/ISTAS48451.2019.8937920

O'Neil, C. (2016). *Weapons of math destruction: How big data increases inequality and threatens democracy*. New York, NY: Crown Publishers.

Ortigosa, A., Carro, R. M., & Quiroga, J. I. (2014). Predicting user personality by mining social interactions in Facebook. *Journal of Computer and System Sciences*, *80*(1), 57–71. doi:10.1016/J.JCSS.2013.03.008

Perez, S. (2019). Over a quarter of US adults now own a smart speaker, typically an Amazon Echo. Retrieved from https://techcrunch.com/2019/03/08/over-a-quarter-of-u-s-adults-now-own-a-smart-speaker-typically-an-amazon-echo/

Purkiss, S. L. S., Perrewé, P. L., Gillespie, T. L., Mayes, B. T., & Ferris, G. R. (2006). Implicit sources of bias in employment interview judgments and decisions. *Organizational Behavior and Human Decision Processes*, *101*(2), 152–167. doi:10.1016/j.obhdp.2006.06.005

Rastogi, A., Pati, S. P., Krishnan, T. N., & Krishnan, S. (2018). Causes, contingencies, and consequences of disengagement at work: An integrative literature review. *Human Resource Development Review*, *17*(1), 62–94. doi:10.1177/1534484317754160

Rogelberg, S. (2006). *Encyclopedia of industrial and organizational psychology.* London: SAGE Publications.

Sackett, P. R. (2007). Revisiting the origins of the typical-maximum performance distinction. *Human Performance, 20*(3), 179–185. doi:10.1080/08959280701332968

Sandy, C. J., Gosling, S. D., & Durant, J. (2013). Predicting consumer behavior and media preferences: The comparative validity of personality traits and demographic variables. *Psychology and Marketing, 30*(11), 937–949. doi:10.1002/mar.20657

Schmitt, N. (2014). Personality and cognitive ability as predictors of effective performance at work. *Annual Review of Organizational Psychology and Organizational Behavior, 1*(1), 45–65. doi:10.1146/annurev-orgpsych-031413-091255

Schwartz, O. (2019). In 2016, Microsoft's racist chatbot revealed the dangers of online conversation. Retrieved from https://spectrum.ieee.org/tech-talk/artificial-intelligence/machine-learning/in-2016-microsofts-racist-chatbot-revealed-the-dangers-of-online-conversation

Schwartz, A. H., Eichstaedt, J. C., Dziurzynski, L., Kern, M. L., Seligman, M. E. P., Ungar, L. H., … Stillwell, D. (2013). Toward personality insights from language exploration in social media. *AAAI Spring Symposium Series*, 72–79. Retrieved from http://sentiment.christopherpotts.net/code-data/

Siege, E. (2015). *Predictive analytic: The power to predict who will click, buy, lie, or die.* Hoboken, NJ: John Wiley & Sons. doi:10.1002/9781119172536

Society for Human Resource Management. (2017). Using social media for talent acquisition. Retrieved from https://

www.shrm.org/hr-today/trends-and-forecasting/research-and-surveys/pages/social-media-recruiting-screening-2015.aspx

Sorenson, S., & Garman, K. (2013). How to tackle U.S. employees' stagnating engagement. Retrieved from https://news.gallup.com/businessjournal/162953/tackle-employees-stagnating-engagement.aspx

Spiggle, T. (2020). Coronavirus silver lining: A better work-life balance? Retrieved from https://www.forbes.com/sites/tomspiggle/2020/10/14/coronavirus-silver-lining-a-better-work-life-balance/?sh=c9aafe01fc29

Strouther, D. (2020). Data reveals 60% of people want to stay at home after COVID-19. Retrieved from https://www.adzooma.com/blog/working-from-home/

Trahan, L. H., Stuebing, K. K., Fletcher, J. M., & Hiscock, M. (2014). The Flynn effect: A meta-analysis. *Psychological Bulletin, 140*(5), 1332–1360. doi:10.1037/a0037173

Twidale, M. B., Blake, C., & Gant, J. (2013). Towards a data literate citizenry. *IConference 2013 Proceedings*, 247–257. doi:10.9776/13189

Wernimont, P. F., & Campbell, J. P. (1968). Signs, samples, and criteria. *Journal of Applied Psychology, 52*(5), 372–376. doi:10.1037/h0026244

Zielinski, D. (2020). Addressing artificial intelligence-based hiring concerns. Retrieved from https://www.shrm.org/hr-today/news/hr-magazine/summer2020/pages/artificial-intelligence-based-hiring-concerns.aspx

3

DIGITAL INTERVIEWS

VIDEO INTERVIEWS AND VIDEO ANALYTICS

Video interviews are arguably the most impactful, and most widely adapted, recruitment innovation of the last years. They first appeared in the early 2000s when webcams became widely available, with early providers sending webcams out to candidates to enable them to take the video interview. Since then, video interviews have fundamentally transformed not only the candidate experience but also the ability and flexibility of organizations to quickly interview candidates across locations. The option to interview remotely and do away with travel reimbursement, room bookings, and complex scheduling has fundamentally changed the way organizations and recruiters handle volumes in their selection funnels. More candidates can interview than would have ever been possible with in person interviews. The logistical and economic advantages of video interviews are obvious. But the most significant innovation in video interviews was yet to arrive: video analytics. Thanks to rapid advances in machine learning and machine vision, and the emergence of computational psychometrics, video interviews today hold an astonishing promise. The ability to automatically screen and profile a practically limitless number of candidates, generating a pre-selected list for time stretched recruiters to review. Matched with video analytics, video interviews promise to automate the recruitment interview. Apart from automation, video analytics offer a structured and data-based method to enhance recruiter decision-making. Algorithms can label interviews with relevant information that might be difficult for recruiters to detect, and might help avoid human biases and inter-rater differences that frequently occur during interview evaluation.

Video analytics today take two distinct forms: (1). Profiling psychometric traits relevant in job performance, such as personality or motivation. In this form they can be thought of as equivalent to psychometric assessments. (2). directly predicting job performance or another desired outcome such as retention or hiring outcome. The second type of profiling is new to the HR world, and to individual differences research which traditionally measure psychometric traits that in turn relate to job performance, rather than directly predicting job performance. In both cases, language as well as nonverbal behavioral cues might be used as inputs for prediction models.

There is no question that technological innovation and practical advantages (first, the spread of web cam usage, then the widespread availability of machine learning algorithms) have driven the development of video interviews. But there is compelling scientific backing for their use too. First, the method of interviewing itself has been extensively studied. Structured interviews are one of the scientifically most valid selection methods. Structured being the key word – only when videos are standardized and questions carefully curated to tease out job relevant skills do they produce notable advantages for identifying top candidates. Second, individual differences are one of the best researched and most robust psychological constructs, with decades of publications

identifying traits and characteristics that predict job performance and other desirable behaviors at work (Barrick &
Mount, 1991). Traditionally measured using self-report
questionnaires, personality is defined as behavioral tendencies and preferences, and as such is reflected in everyday
actions, including language use and nonverbal behaviors
(Maltby, Day, & Macaskill, 2017). Indeed, the emerging field
of computational psychometrics has, over the last decade,
produced compelling evidence that data sources included in
video interviews can generate accurate personality profiles
(Hickman, Bosch, et al., 2021; Suen, Hung, & Lin, 2019).
This science is applied as the basis of video interview
assessments.

However, scientific research on the use of video analytics
for selection is yet to catch up with their application in
industry. Few studies look at video analytics as selection
methods, and those that do tend to be restricted to hiring
manager decision-making, rather than job performance
(Wilson & Daugherty, 2018). Ample studies show that the
mechanisms underlying video analytics work and individual
differences theory provide a framework with which to justify
why interview behavior should be related to job performance.
But there is a lack of studies showing how video analytics
impact HR relevant outcomes, such as diversity, or whether
they meet the stringent psychometric properties required for
selection tools.

ADVANTAGES FOR TALENT IDENTIFICATION: WHAT IS NEW?

Looking beyond the modern tech and new user experiences,
video interviews and video analytics have the potential to
fundamentally change recruitment and selection practices.

Two points are of particular importance: (1) video interview technology enables the implementation of scientifically validated, best practice recruitment tools at scale and (2) video analytics might improve the quality of the tools themselves.

Video interviews and video analytics introduce structure into the recruitment process at scale: Structured recruitment processes are better at identifying talent and lead to more diverse hires (Mccarthy, Van Iddekinge, & Campion, 2010). By introducing formal structure, the evaluation of candidates is standardized, reducing the influence of circumstance, personal bias, and existing networks on selection decisions (Levashina, Hartwell, Morgeson, & Campion, 2014).

The two elements of structured recruitment processes currently implemented with video interviews and video analytics are structured interviews, which are standardized in both the content and the evaluation through practices such as customizing questions to fit the job and consistency with the interviewer (Campion, Palmer, & Campion, 1997), and standardized psychometric assessments such as personality and intelligence tests. Standardized interviews and psychometric assessments are the most consistent and reliable predictors of job performance and other career-related outcomes (Barrick & Mount, 1991; Schmitt, 2014; Wiesner & Cronshaw, 1988). Decades of research document that they outperform assessment centers, job tryouts, reference checks, job experience, and other popular selection methods (Schmidt & Hunter, 1998). Importantly, structured interviews outperform unstructured interviews, indicating that the standardization of interview questions and structured evaluation of answers is key to successfully detecting talent during interviews (McDaniel, Whetzel, Schmidt, & Maurer, 1994; Schmidt & Hunter, 1998; Wiesner & Cronshaw, 1988). Video interviews are structured: all candidates answer the same questions, which are designed to elicit job relevant competencies. Video analytics replicate psychometric assessments: they are used to profile individual differences in applicant behavior during the interview to either predict personality traits related to job performance or predict job performance directly.

Structured Interviews and Standardized Analysis at Scale

Research has consistently demonstrated that structured employment interviews are valid for predicting job performance criteria (Campion et al., 1997; McDaniel et al., 1994). Meta-analysis of studies spanning 100 years demonstrates that structured interviews have nearly unrivaled validity compared with other common selection methods in predicting job relevant outcomes ($r = 0.51$ and 0.58, respectively, Schmidt, Oh, & Shaffer, 2016; Schmidt & Hunter, 1998).

Despite the scientific evidence for their validity, structured interviews are not widely implemented. A survey of 750 people found that 65% of the companies respondents were employed by did not use structured interviews (The Predictive Index, 2020). There are significant barriers to their consistent implementation, including time pressure, lack of process, and lack of expertise. Structured interviews feel less personal and take longer to plan than unstructured interviews, can be seen as rigid and inflexible, and may not complement the cognitive style of the interviewer (Macan, 2009). Training individuals on interview protocol is often expensive (Chauhan, 2019). Even with extensive training, human raters make inferences that are not job related, bring idiosyncratic biases to the evaluation process, lack the ability to recall job-related details of the interview, and lack accuracy in making criterion-related judgments and decisions that predict success on the job (Campion et al., 1997). However, consistency of content and consistency of administration or process are crucial to achieve validity of structured interviews (Campion et al., 1997; Leva-shina et al., 2014). To alleviate issues associated with human evaluations, organizations must invest substantial time and money into developing structured and standardized interview processes (Bohnet, 2016).

Video interview analytics offer an alternative to extensive training and human controls. They offer the technology to implement structured interviewing while doing away with their costly implementation and minimizing the risk of human evaluator bias and inconsistencies. Indeed, computer scoring of video interviews provides comparable ratings to human evaluators (Campion, Campion, Campion, & Reider, 2016). For example, video analytics providers Aon and Hirevue report convergent validities of around $r = 0.5$ between human and algorithm video ratings, with validities depending on the competency measured as well as the interview question types used (HireVue, 2021; Liu, Bartkoski, Brandt, Theys, & Lobbe, 2021). Automated assessments of interviews success-fully replicate human expert judgments without having a negative impact on diversity. Additionally, the automated assessment system leads to positive financial impact and reduced costs for the company (Campion et al., 2016).

Better Data

Video interviews deliver radically different data, and possibil-ities for analyzing that data, compared to traditional recruit-ment processes. Importantly, the data provided go beyond self-reported questionnaire answers provided on fixed scales that are typically used in psychometric assessment. These richer data could deliver more accurate assessments of candidates (more on this in the section A, Rich Source of Data).

Secondly, these rich data can be used to directly predict work performance, rather than predicting traits related to work performance. This is particularly interesting for job roles where reliable performance data are available, and were hundreds or thousands of people work in comparable job roles, such as call centers or customer service roles. Indeed, manually rated video interview performance significantly related to self-reported job performance based on appraisals in a recent study (Gorman, Robinson, & Gamble, 2018). However, few studies are available on the link between automatically scored interview performance and subsequent job performance.

And finally, structured interviews are evaluated by human raters, who are only able to pay attention to a subset of information provided by the candidate during the interview. In addition, personal biases and circumstance will play into evaluations, and these will vary across human raters (Derous, Buijsrogge, Roulin, & Duyck, 2016). Such individual interviewer effects are eliminated with standardized video analytics, which are applied to each candidate in the same way. This does not mean that video analytics are free of bias, but they do deliver a highly standardized evaluation method.

Monitoring and Adjusting Decision Making

In addition, the bias produced by automated scoring can be monitored and adjusted on a large scale. This is where video interviews are fundamentally different from human ratings, and even assessments. The growing field of algorithmic fairness is increasingly developing methods to adjust algorithm-based scores to minimize bias and equalize decision-making across groups. For example, monitoring and rectifying any biases in algorithms by using diverse and accurate datasets to train the algorithms and removing any features that result in bias (HireVue, 2019; Malta AI, 2019). This is a powerful tool to reduce bias instantly and at scale – compared to the resource heavy and mostly ineffective tools for reducing bias in human decision makers (Kawakami et al., 2005, 2007).

Initial evidence from application is positive, with Unilever reporting a 16% increase in diversity of new hires, in terms of both ethnicity and gender, after teaming with interview assessment provider HireVue (HireVue, 2017). However, there is a lack of academic studies exploring the effect of video interviews and analytics on fairness in the recruitment process.

VIDEO INTERVIEW ANALYTICS: A RICH SOURCE OF DATA

Instead of predefined answers to specific questions, video interviews generate large amounts of initially unstructured data. For video interview analytics, or an automated evaluation of these videos, these data must be processed and structured. It can then be analyzed and used to score candidates against relevant outcome criteria such as personality, competency, or job performance. Both verbal and nonverbal behavior can be extracted from the video material. The following section described data features that can be extracted from video interviews, and how they link to theoretically and empirical relevant constructs in employee selection. The list is not exhaustive – video interview data enable the extraction of many different types of datapoints, including facial recognition or analysis of background images. However, these types of data either lack theoretical underpinnings or raise ethical concerns and are, based on our understanding, not common in the applied use of video interviews in recruitment and selection today.

Words

An extensive body of literature links language use to personality and individual attributes (Kern et al., 2014; Pennebaker & King, 1999; Yarkoni, 2010). Personality describes behavioral tendencies and preferences of individuals, and is one of the best studied and most consistent predictors of job performance (Barrick & Mount, 1991; Judge, Higgins, Thoresen, & Barrick, 1999). Typically measured through self-report questionnaires, advances in machine learning and the wide availability of free text data resulted in a wave of research studies demonstrating that personality can be predicted from language use in different contexts (Lambiotte & Kosinski, 2014; Schwartz et al., 2013). This includes as Twitter or personal blogs (Schwartz et al., 2013). These prediction algorithms show moderate accuracy in predicting the Big Five personality traits from language use ($r = 0.37$ for conscientiousness; Park et al., 2015). In addition, machine learning–based predictions of personality from language outperformed human judges when comparing the convergence of inter-judge agreement for machine ($r = 0.62$) versus human judgments ($r = 0.38$) (Bleidorn & Hopwood, 2019). For example, machine learning algorithm predictions of Big Five traits are more accurate ($r = 0.56$ vs $r = 0.49$) than friends' judgments of Big Five traits via a 100-item questionnaire (Youyou, Kosinski, & Stillwell, 2015).

This indicates that automated scoring algorithms can extract personality from text with a reasonable level of accuracy, and might thereby be able to offer additional valuable information for recruiters if used to analyze video interview data. However, video interviews contain spoken words rather than written text, adding an additional layer of complexity: text needs to be transcribed before it can be analyzed. To date, few studies have looked at the predictive validity of language transcribed from video in predicting self-reported personality. One available study indicates that accuracies might be lower than for models that use written text, which might be a result of additional error introduced by transcription (between $r = 0.1$ and $r = 0.21$; Hickman, Bosch, et al., 2021). Indeed, the same study showed moderate to high predictive validity for interviewer-rated personality based on video interviews (between $r = 0.27$ and $r = 0.65$; Hickman, Bosch, et al., 2021). This indicates that prediction models perform well when approximating interviewer ratings of interviewee personality, even with the error introduced from transcription.

Natural Language Processing: From Words to Features

Transcription

Spoken word from video interviews is transcribed to obtain text that can then be used in subsequent analysis. This is done using transcription algorithms such as those used in voice commands for mobile phones or in automated subtitles. The transcription accuracy for most providers is reasonably high and is measured by the Word Error Rate which takes into account substitutions (replacing the correct word with an incorrect one), deletions (missing transcription), and insertions (transcribing a nonexistent word). Word error rates of around 17% are typical, but vary dramatically depending on the dataset. Aspects such as low volume, accent, speech style, background noise, and sound quality can affect transcription accuracy. Researchers have demonstrated that word error rates can vary considerably between groups, with male and white voices typically transcribed at higher accuracy (Bajorek, 2019). Consequently, transcription algorithms present a source of bias because they tend to introduce more error into the data of interviewees belonging to specific groups.

Bag of Words

Bag of words approaches are typical in Natural Language Processing, and the simplest way of representing text for analysis by machine learning and other models. For bag of word approaches, only the included words are retained, while grammatical structure and order of the text are disregarded. Imagine a simple list of all words mentioned in a body of text, with a number counting the times a given word has appeared. Each word becomes a variable, or feature, that can be entered into a prediction algorithm and used in subsequent analysis. Despite their simplicity, bag of word approaches yield good results and are frequently used in Natural Language Processing. They do, however, have obvious flaws in ignoring the context of words. These flaws have only recently been addressed by innovations in Natural Language Processing (see "Context" below).

Language Use and Content

Based on bag of word approaches, several systems have been developed to extract additional information from text transcripts. These approaches seek to attach additional labels to words included in a transcript. Labels typically relate to word choice, meaning, or language use. They may also include meaning categories that words are scored against using extensive dictionaries (i.e., Dictionaries containing all words relating to "family" or "oney"). Labels generated with the help of these systems can then be entered into any subsequent analysis in the same way that single words would be in a bag of words approach. Examples of such language use and content systems include:

- The General Inquirer, with over 400 parameters including categories such as over- or understatement, words referring to specific institutions (academic, economic, legal, etc.) or cognitive orientations (thinking, knowing, solving, etc.) (Stone, Dunphi, Marshall, & Olgilvie, 1966).

- The Natural Language Toolkit which categorizes word types, for example, into pronouns related to the self, others, etc. (Loper & Bird, 2002).

- The Linguistic Inquiry and Word Count (LIWC) classifies word use along 93 features including language metrics, function words, grammar, and meaning groups (Pennebaker, Boyd, Jordan, & Blackburn, 2015). The LIWC includes several feature categories based on dictionaries: function words, affect words, social words, cognitive processes, perceptual processes, biological processes, core drives and needs, time orientation, relativity, personal concerns, informal speech, and punctuation.

Context

Context has historically been a notoriously difficult problem in Natural Language Processing. Bag of word approaches ignore any meaning and context, analyzing each word in isolation. Language use and content systems as described above have gone some way in adding a layer of meaning to bag of word approaches, but are limited in scope and require theory driven and manual development of word categories and dictionaries. The Bidirectional Encoder Representations from Transformer (BERT; Feng, Yang, Cer, Arivazhagan, & Wang, 2020) has fundamentally changed this. BERT is a Natural Language Processing pretraining algorithm that takes into account the context in which a word occurs and is thereby thought to account for meaning relationships between words. BERT, unlike bag of word approaches, would be able to account for the fact that "running" in "running a business" or "running a company" means something similar, but that "running" in "running a marathon" would mean something different. BERT has performed well in solving typical Natural

Language Processing problems and may enhance the accuracy of models inferring job relevant attributes such as personality based on video interview text.

Nonverbal Behavior

Compared to words and language, nonverbal data and its relationship to personality or other job relevant outcomes are less well studied. There are also fewer off the shelf algorithms are available to extract and analysis nonverbal data. Indeed, some studies to date that compare the predictive power of nonverbal over verbal data conclude that verbal data have relatively more predictive power (Biel, Tsiminaki, Dines, & Gatica-Perez, 2013; Hickman, Bosch, et al., 2021). This means that including nonverbal behavior in video interview analytics, at least with the methods commonly employed today, is unlikely to add much performance to a prediction algorithm when words are already included.

Nonetheless, in practice, nonverbal behavioral features may be collected during video interviews and used to analyze candidates. A theoretical reason for their inclusion also exists. Much of human communication is nonverbal, and humans use nonverbal behavior to form impressions of others (Ambady & Rosenthal, 1993). Nonverbal behavior affects how interviewees are perceived and evaluated: In a study using manual coding, interviewer ratings of applicants were affected by their nonverbal behavior and verbal content exhibited during the interview (Rasmussen, 1984). Both types of behaviors interact such that ratings of applicant performance are higher when good verbal content is paired with high levels of nonverbal behavior, and lower when high levels are paired with poor verbal content (Rasmussen, 1984). These findings are replicated in studies using automatic extraction of behavioral cues from videos of interviewees and interviewers, where these cues explain 36% of variance in hiring decisions, and are more predictive of hiring decision compared to psychometric questionnaires (Nguyen, Frauendorfer, Mast, & Gatica-Perez, 2014). Nonverbal behaviors might affect interviewer ratings because they offer personality cues to interviewers. Indeed, nonverbal cues directly influence the personality judgments made by others (Friedman & Miller-Herringer, 1991).

Automated systems for extracting nonverbal behaviors demonstrate some accuracy in predicting personal characteristics, with studies showing that audio characteristics and facial expressions are predictive of underlying personality (Carbonneau, Granger, Attabi, & Gagnon, 2017; Nguyen & Gatica-Perez, 2015; Sarkar, Bhatia, Agarwal, & Li, 2014). Nonverbal cues automatically extracted from online video resumes explain 27% of variance in first impression ratings of extraversion, and 20% of variance in social and communication skills (Nguyen & Gatica-Perez, 2016). When taking into account both facial expression and vocal analysis, other ratings of personality traits were classified correctly in 40%–63% of cases, depending on the trait (Rupasinghe, Gunawardena, Shujan, & Atukorale, 2017). Speech clips achieve accuracies of 70%–80% in classifying people's Big Five personality traits (Mohammadi, Origlia, Filippone, & Vinciarelli, 2012; Mohammadi & Vinciarelli, 2012). Speech signals such as rate, energy, pitch, and silent intervals are successfully distinguished between high and low extraverts in 86% of cases (Kwon, YeonChoeh, & Lee, 2013).

Given that human raters take into account nonverbal behaviors, prediction algorithms that seek to replicate human ratings should benefit from the inclusion of nonverbal behavior. Yet, in video interview data, the contribution verbal behavior outweighs that of nonverbal behavior for most personality traits when predicting interviewer ratings of the Big Five personality traits (Hickman, Bosch, et al., 2021). This might be a reflection of the fact that currently available methods for the automatic analysis of nonverbal behavior are less established than those for speech or text, which benefit from our system of written language as well as the active field of Natural Language Processing. Examples of systems to extract nonverbal data from video interviews include:

Spectral Audio Characteristics

Feature learning algorithms can extract audio features such as rate of speech, pitch, intonation, range, gaps in speech, and repetition of speech. These algorithms can be designed specifically to extract audio variables related to the Big Five personality traits (generating 50 variables in this example, for details see Carbonneau et al., 2017).

Facial Action Units

Facial action units describe facial movements within the "Facial Action Coding" system which is based on Ekman's study of emotion and his system of six basic emotions (Ekman & Friesen, 1978; Ekman & Rosenberg, 2012). The coding system analyzes 64 different facial action units (e.g., head tilt) and generates over 250 individual variables, including brow or chin raise, nose wrinkle, or other facial movements (Tian, Kanade, & Conn, 2001). Ekman's emotion framework has been criticized for its oversimplification of intricate human emotional processes, and the ability to diagnose emotions based on facial movements is equally problematic (Barrett, Adolphs, Marsella, Martinez, & Pollak, 2019). However, facial action units do not require the validity of Ekman's theory but rather offer a computerized system to label micromovements of the face. These movements then form the basis of subsequent analysis, such as predicting personality.

Much like the bag of word approaches discussed earlier, facial action units and other nonverbal behaviors are, when using the methods available today, analyzed without context. A high-pitched voice or an agitated facial expression occurring anywhere during the video interview will be labeled the same, regardless of the conversational context. Infusing context into the analysis of nonverbal behavior may help improve prediction models.

VIDEO INTERVIEW ANALYTICS FOR THE BETTER? FAIRNESS AND ACCURACY ACROSS GROUPS

Video interviews offer practical and financial advantages over in person interviews. With distributed teams and remote working, they have become a necessity for many employers (Schawbel, 2020). This alone makes the technology popular in application. We have also seen that, if implemented correctly, video interviewing technology can help recruiters maintain a structured selection process. This increases fairness by reducing the effect of interviewer bias and variation across interviews and allows for a standardized comparison of candidates. In both of these applications, interviews are evaluated by human raters and the role of video interviewing technology is to facilitate the coming together of interviews and candidates, as well as to support the evaluation work of interviewers in implementing best practices for structured interviewing. The fairness of video interview evaluations and recruitment decisions made will be based on the quality of human decision making.

This section will focus on the fairness and accuracy of video interview analytics: When algorithms are used to evaluate or rate video interviews, the fairness of those evaluations and ultimately recruitment decisions will depend, at least in part, on the fairness of the algorithms. Often, this is discussed in terms of the risks introduced by algorithmic evaluations of video interviews (Bogen, 2019; Kahn, 2021; Raghavan & Barocas, 2019). Automatically evaluated video interviews are presented as an example of machines taking over our lives, and as a source of discrimination and a worsening of the current status of recruitment (Köchling, Riazy, Wehner, & Simbeck, 2021). This discussion is necessary and algorithms that make decisions about humans must be carefully audited. However, the benefits of algorithmic video interview evaluations equally warrant attention: Decades of research in individual differences and occupational psychology (1) show that structured recruitment processes and in particular structured interviews lead to fairer and higher quality hiring decisions (Levashina et al., 2014), and (2) that screening for specific abilities, competencies, and personality helps recruit candidates who are likely to have the best job performance (Hogan, Hogan, & Roberts, 1996). Both are supported and potentially enhanced by using video interview analytics.

Research shows that behavioral observations such as language use and nonverbal behaviors are good indicators of personality and other work relevant traits, and that human evaluations of video interviews can be approximated by algorithms (Campion et al., 2016; Hickman, Bosch, et al., 2021). Paired with technological advances, this opens a wide range of possibilities to develop and deploy algorithms to evaluate video interviews and support recruiter decision making. Even though video interview–based algorithms are new, the use of algorithms to support recruiter decision making is not. Psychometric assessments that score candidates along work relevant traits have been part of recruitment processes for decades. As a result, guidelines and best practices for the use of assessments in recruitment are in place (e.g., American Educational Research Association, American

Psychological Association, & National Council on Measure-ment in Education, 1999; Equal Employment Opportunity Commission, 1978; Society for Industrial and Organizational Psychology, 2018). Automatic evaluations of video interviews, or video interview analytics, are a new type of psychometric assessment. They must therefore be executed within those guidelines and best practices. Existing guidelines offer a valuable starting point in evaluating the fairness of video interview analytics. At the same time, the technologies underlying video interview analytics, in particular machine learning scoring models, are new to psychometric assessments, posing limitations on existing regulation.

The following section will highlight two guiding principles of particular relevance for video interview analytics:

- What is the assessment measuring and why? Content val-idity: The assessment needs to measure competencies and traits relevant to the job role or organizational context in question. Convergent validity studies must demonstrate that the assessment is indeed measuring what it claims to measure, by showing that it results in similar scores as other assessments of the same trait.

- Does the assessment work, i.e. how well does it measure what it is supposed to measure? Convergent, predictive, and test retest reliability attest the quality of an assessment.

- Is the assessment fair? Extensive adverse impact testing should be part of any assessment development process. Where artificial intelligence and machine learning are used to generate input, or features, for scoring models, these features must also be evaluated for differences in accuracy across groups.

Psychometric Standards: Considerations for Video Interview Analytics

Content validity is a core principle in psychometric tests, and is of particular importance for tests used in the employee selection context. A test, metric, or assessment used to evaluate job candidates needs to be relevant to performance in the respective job. Typically, psychometric test measures well-defined psychological concepts such as personality or intelligence. An extensive body of literature demonstrates their relevance in job performance (Barrick & Mount, 1991; Kuncel, Ones, & Sackett, 2010; Schmidt & Hunter, 1998; Schmidt et al., 2016; Schmitt, 2014). This can be further established with local validation studies. Structured interviews are carefully designed such that questions address core competencies required in the job role (Campion et al., 1997). Competencies are typically defined through a job analysis that details the requirements for and skills of successful candidates in a given role (Bach, 2005). These processes ensure that assessments put in front of candidates measure role relevant attributes.

Algorithmic analysis of video interview assessments typically replicates either psychometric test of psychological constructs such as personality, or the evaluation of competencies based on structured interviews (Campion et al., 2016; Hickman, Bosch, et al., 2021). However, video interviews can also be used to score other types of outcomes such as job performance or hiring decision, or a mix of all of the above. These types of models are less well studied in the academic literature and may lack some of the theoretical underpinnings of models that measure psychological traits or competencies. A careful evaluation of the measured outcome is recommended if using models of this type. For example, models predicting job performance will depend entirely on the quality of job performance data available. Any flaws in job evaluations will be replicated and feature into hiring decisions. Such models may also be unsuitable for hiring a "new" type of candidate that has historically either not been hired or unable to perform well at the company because job performance data will only reflect current or historic employees and environments.

Types of video interview analytics and main considerations:

1. Predict human ratings (or interviewer ratings) of job relevant competencies or traits. These models replicate and automate structured interviews. Structured interviews improve fairness and quality outcomes compared to unstructured interviews and are one of the most effective methods for predicting job performance (Schmidt & Hunter, 1998).

2. Predict self-reported psychological traits such as personality that are related to job performance. These models replicate psychometric tests or assessments traditionally conducted using questionnaires. They are well supported by research and measure stable traits that consistently predict job performance.

3. Predict job performance data or other organizational outcomes: These models represent a new type of selection test and warrant careful evaluation of the job performance data. They lack a theoretical underpinning and vulnerable to measuring irrelevant, undesirable, or circumstantial factors.

Convergent validity is typically measured by the correlation between a new test and an established test of a given construct. With traditional tests, this meant correlating one test score with another. For video interview analytics, convergent validity typically is reported as the correlation between the predicted score and the actual score, or as the model performance: For example, if using video interviews to predict scores on a personality test, convergent validity will be reported as the correlation between the predicted scores the algorithm produces and scores on the personality test. This means that in the context of video interview analytics, convergent validity describes model performance. Additional metrics may be used to evaluate model performance depending on the artificial intelligence or machine learning models used, including F1 scores or area under the curve. Correlations have the advantage of being easily interpretable by those familiar with psychometric tests. Convergent validities reported for tests predicting self-reported personality traits from video interviews are around $r = 0.2$ (Hickman, Saef, et al., 2021). And for tests predicting human ratings of personality or competencies are around $r = 0.5$ (Hickman, Saef, et al., 2021). Why these differences in model performance, or convergent validity, exist and which models are more predictive of job performance is currently not well studied.

Reliability or test retest reliability describes whether a test produces similar scores if taken twice by the same individual, typically within a few weeks or days. Assuming that personality and competencies are relatively stable, and that a job candidate is as equally well or not well suited for a job when interviewing on a Monday as they will be when interviewing again on the Friday, video interview analytics should produce reliable scores. Few published studies are available that describe the test retest reliability of video interview analytics. Such studies could provide reassurance that the open ended format of video interviews is able to produce reliable metrics, comparable to the high reliability of psychometric tests. Given the lack of information, there is a concern that nonverbal behaviors might influence models in an undesirable way, or that providers use datapoints that are entirely circumstantial in their analytics models, like screen backgrounds or outfits. Such variables would result in a low test retest reliability. Journalists have anecdotally tested the robustness of video interview scores by completing interviews in different settings and outfits, but giving the same verbal responses. Their results showed a troubling difference between scores (Fergus, 2021). While this offers an insight into test retest reliability, it is not a substitute for providers reporting test retest correlations.

Predictive validity describes whether scores on an assessment correlate with the desired outcome. For example, whether personality scores generated based on a video interview taken at job applications predict job performance two years on. Predictive validity provides a valuable indicator that an assessment is measuring job relevant characteristics. In traditional assessments, job performance or other metrics are typically used to evaluate predictive validity. Job performance metrics are not used to inform the scoring key of the assessment itself. Because of their predictive scoring models, video interview analytics lend themselves to the retro-fitting of scoring models to approximate job performance. Video interview scoring models can also be designed from the start to directly predict job performance. Models that directly predict job performance are likely to outperform those that predict psychological traits or competencies, and will therefore look like they offer the best option to identify candidates that will perform well. However, caution is needed. Job performance data are notoriously flawed, context dependent, and difficult to compare across managers, roles, or functions (Singh, Darwish, & Potočnik, 2016). Often, performance data are based on subjective human ratings with little controls for biases and individual raters (Prendergast & Topel, 1993). In practice, sample sizes of job performance data are limited, further exaggerating theses effects. Any models predicting a flawed outcome will themselves be flawed. Apart from flawed outcome data and limited sample sizes, direct predictions of job performance are limiting in that they will result in the recruitment of people who will be similar to current employees and perform well in the historical or current context of the company. Where companies are recruiting for new functions, undergoing significant changes, or looking to diversify their teams, hiring for current and historic job performance might not be the best option. Performance-based models also lack a layer of exploitability that competencies and personality trait models provide, and cannot rely on past research validating the theoretical and empirical validity of competencies and traits in predicting job performance.

Adverse Impact and Accuracy of Video Interview Algorithms for Different Groups

In recruitment and selection, fairness is typically assessed in terms of adverse impact: The degree to which one group scores consistently higher (or lower) than another group on an assessment used to make hiring decisions (Hausdorf, Leblanc, & Chawla, 2003; Risavy & Hausdorf, 2011). Video interview analytics, when applied as assessments to support employment decisions, therefore, must demonstrate that the scores they produce do not result in differing scores for relevant groups, which in practice typically include ethnic, gender, and age groups but extend to other groups such as sexual orientation, religion, and disability as well.

This section will focus on two aspects that are unique to video interview analytics compared to traditional assessments:

- The adequate diversity of training datasets used to develop the scoring algorithm.

- The features used in video analytics or the data extracted from video interviews.

First, video interview analytics use machine learning and artificial intelligence models that learn to predict a given outcome (a psychological trait, competencies, job perfor-mance,...) based on the data provided. This means that the training data represent a limiting factor for model accuracy or generalizability (Domingos, 2012). The model will only be capable of accurately scoring video interviews that look like those contained in the dataset. Therefore, the training dataset must be representative of the candidate population. Training datasets need to contain a range of ages, genders, ethnicities as well as other relevant factors such as job level, experience, cultural background, accent, and opinions. For example, nonverbal behavior varies between ethnic minorities and majorities (Vrij, Dragt, & Koppelaar, 1992). If an algorithm is based on a sample of ethnic majority, it will be less accurate in scoring the nonverbal behavior of ethnic minorities.

Second, any artificial intelligence or machine learning algorithms used to produce features later used to score video interviews must themselves comply with adverse impact standards. For example, spoken word is transcribed into text before it is used in video interview analytics. The algorithms used for transcription should have similar accuracies for members of different groups, and should not consistently result in lower scores for members of specific groups. Mea-sures of accuracy for different groups are a typical metric used when evaluating machine learning models (Corbett-Davies & Goel, 2018). Research shows that both transcription and face analysis algorithms tend to perform better for white people and males than they do for people of color and females. Transcription accuracies vary for gender and ethnicity (Bajorek, 2019). Face recognition accuracy varies with skin tone and gender (Buolamwini, 2018). Voice recognition accuracy varies with accent (Palanica, Thommandram, Lee, Li, & Fossat, 2019; Tatman, 2017; Tatman & Kasten, 2017) as well as gender (Mason & Thompson, 1993; Tatman, 2017).

SUMMARY OF PRACTICAL IMPLICATIONS

Video interviews have the potential to deliver massive time savings for the recruitment process, introduce structure, and enhance the fairness and quality of recruiter decision making, as well as increase response rates due to better user experience and flexibility compared to in person interviews. This means organizations can cut costs and increase their chances to get top candidates to apply.

However, the true potential of video interviews lies in the automated review of large amounts of candidates, delivered through video analytics, or video assessments. This enables companies, even with small HR teams, to evaluate large pools of applicants, thereby increasing chances to discover top candidates. Automated video evaluations can also enhance recruiter decisions and help debias the selection process. For those who are already overwhelmed with the cost of reviewing applications, video analytics offer significant costs savings compared to manual review.

Efficiency gains compared to analog interviews are also made in processing time, and therefore time to hire. This again is critical to securing top candidates and minimizing productivity loss from unfilled roles. When delivered through platforms that integrate video interviews with additional recruitment funnel steps, time savings are made in integration with providers and streamlining separate recruitment process steps.

Beyond these operational advantages, video interviews offer the hope of a fair and valid selection process that delivers a diverse and talented workforce. For the first time, it is technically possible to define and monitor standardized selection processes across several steps, and, more importantly, to adjust and correct bias in decision making on a large scale and in (near to) real time.

First academic and case studies provide evidence that this hope is translating into reality, albeit unsolved problems with both the data and techniques underlying video interviews. Research and development work in the coming years should focus on defining and tackling these problems.

REFERENCES

Ambady, N., & Rosenthal, R. (1993). Half a minute: Predicting teacher evaluations from thin slices of nonverbal behavior and physical attractiveness. *Journal of Personality and Social Psychology*, *64*(3), 431–441. doi:10.1037/0022-3514.64.3.431

American Educational Research Association, American Psychological Association, & National Council on Measurement in Education. (1999). Standards for the educational and psychological testing. Retrieved from https://www.aera.net/Portals/38/1999%Standards_revised.pdf

Bach, S. (2005). *Managing human resources: Personnel management in transition*. Hoboken, NJ: Blackwell.

Bajorek, J. P. (2019). Voice recognition still has significant race and gender biases. Retrieved from https://hbr.org/2019/05/voice-recognition-still-has-significant-race-and-gender-biases

Barrett, L. F., Adolphs, R., Marsella, S., Martinez, A. M., & Pollak, S. D. (2019). Emotional expressions reconsidered: Challenges to inferring emotion from human facial movements. *Psychological Science in the Public Interest*, *20*(1), 1–68. doi:10.1177/1529100619832930

Barrick, M. R., & Mount, M. K. (1991). The Big Five personality dimensions and job performance: A meta-analysis. *Personnel Psychology*, *44*(1), 1–26. doi:10.1111/j.1744-6570.1991.tb00688.x

Biel, J. -I., Tsiminaki, V., Dines, J., & Gatica-Perez, D. (2013). Hi YouTube! Personality impressions and verbal content in social video. In Proceedings of the 15th ACM on International Conference on Multimodal Interaction (pp. 119–126). doi:10.1145/2522848.2522877

Bleidorn, W., & Hopwood, C. J. (2019). Using machine learning to advance personality assessment and Theory. *Personality and Social Psychology Review*, *23*(2), 190–203. doi:10.1177/1088868318772990

Bogen, M. (2019). All the ways hiring algorithms can introduce bias. Retrieved from https://hbr.org/2019/05/all-the-ways-hiring-algorithms-can-introduce-bias

Bohnet, I. (2016). How to take the bias out of interviews. *Harvard Business Review*, *16*, 1–5. Retrieved from http://cdi.brighamandwomens.org/wp-content/uploads/2020/09/How-to-Take-the-Bias-Out-of-Interviews.pdf

Buolamwini, J. (2018). Gender shades: Intersectional accuracy disparities in commercial gender classification. *Proceedings of Machine Learning Research*, *81*, 1–15. Retrieved from http://proceedings.mlr.press/v81/buolamwini18a/buolamwini18a.pdf

Campion, M. C., Campion, M. A., Campion, E. D., & Reider, M. H. (2016). Initial investigation into computer scoring of candidate essays for personnel selection. *Journal of Applied Psychology*, *101*(7), 958–975. doi:10.1037/APL0000108

Campion, M. A., Palmer, D. K., & Campion, J. E. (1997). A review of structure in the selection interview. *Personnel Psychology*, *50*(3), 655–702. doi:10.1111/j.1744-6570.1997.tb00709.x

Carbonneau, M. A., Granger, E., Attabi, Y., & Gagnon, G. (2017). Feature learning from spectrograms for assessment of personality traits. *IEEE Transactions on Affective Computing*, *11*(1), 25–31.

Chauhan, R. S. (2019). Unstructured interviews: Are they really all that bad? *Human Resource Development International*, 1–14. doi:10.1080/13678868.2019.1603019

Corbett-Davies, S., & Goel, S. (2018). The measure and mismeasure of fairness: A critical review of fair machine learning. Retrieved from http://arxiv.org/abs/1808.00023

Derous, E., Buijsrogge, A., Roulin, N., & Duyck, W. (2016). Why your stigma isn't hired: A dual-process framework of interview bias. *Human Resource Management Review*, *26*(2), 90–111. doi:10.1016/j.hrmr.2015.09.006

Domingos, P. (2012). A few useful things to know about machine learning. *Communications of the ACM*, *55*(10), 78–87. doi:10.1145/2347736.2347755

Ekman, P., & Friesen, W. V. (1978). *The facial action coding system (FACS)*. Consulting psychologist press.

Ekman, P., & Rosenberg, E. L. (2012). *What the face reveals: Basic and applied studies of spontaneous expression using the facial action coding system (FACS)*. Oxford University Press. doi:10.1093/acprof:oso/9780195179644.001.0001

Equal Employment Opportunity Commission. (1978). Uniform guidelines on employee selection procedures. *Federal Register*, *43*(166), 38290–38315.

Feng, F., Yang, Y., Cer, D., Arivazhagan, N., & Wang, W. (2020). Language-agnostic BERT sentence embedding. Retrieved from http://arxiv.org/abs/2007.01852

Fergus, J. (2021). A bookshelf in your job screening video makes you more hirable to AI. Retrieved from https://www.inputmag.com/culture/a-bookshelf-in-your-job-screening-video-makes-you-more-hirable-to-ai

Friedman, H. S., & Miller-Herringer, T. (1991). Nonverbal display of emotion in public and in private: Self-monitoring, personality, and expressive cues. *Journal of Personality and Social Psychology*, *61*(5), 766–775. doi:10.1037/0022-3514.61.5.766

Gorman, C. A., Robinson, J., & Gamble, J. S. (2018). An investigation into the validity of asynchronous web-based video employment-interview ratings. *Consulting Psychology Journal*, *70*(2), 129–146. doi:10.1037/cpb0000102

Hausdorf, P. A., Leblanc, M. M., & Chawla, A. (2003). Cognitive ability testing and employment selection: Does test content relate to adverse impact? *Applied H.R.M. Research*, *7*(2), 41–48. Retrieved from http://applyhrm.asp.radford.edu/2002/ms%207_2_%20hausdorf.pdf

Hickman, L., Bosch, N., Ng, V., Saef, R., Tay, L., & Woo, S. E. (2021). Automated video interview personality assessments: Reliability, validity, and generalizability investigations. *Journal of Applied Psychology*. doi:10.1037/apl0000695

Hickman, L., Saef, R., Ng, V., Woo, S. E., Tay, L., & Bosch, N. (2021). Developing and evaluating language-based machine learning algorithms for inferring applicant personality in video interviews. *Human Resource Management Journal.* doi:10.1111/1748-8583.12356

HireVue. (2017). Unilever finds top talent faster with HireVue assessments. Retrieved from https://www.hirevue.com/case-studies/global-talent-acquisition-unilever-case-study

HireVue. (2019). Bias, AI ethics and the HireVue approach. Retrieved from https://www.hirevue.com/why-hirevue/ethical-ai

HireVue. (2021). Hirevue's assessment science White Paper. Retrieved from https://webapi.hirevue.com/wp-content/uploads/2021/09/2021_08_24_HireVue_Assessment_Science_white_paper-Final-2.pdf?_ga=2.114150791.1884920666.1635767779-2025020875.1635767779

Hogan, R., Hogan, J., & Roberts, B. W. (1996). Personality measurement and employment decisions: Questions and answers. *American Psychologist, 51*(5), 469–477. doi:10.1037/0003-066X.51.5.469

Judge, T. A., Higgins, C. A., Thoresen, C. J., & Barrick, M. R. (1999). The big five personality traits, general mental ability, and career success across the life span. *Personnel Psychology, 52*(3), 621–652. doi:10.1111/j.1744-6570.1999.tb00174.x

Kahn, J. (2021). HireVue stops using facial expressions to assess job candidates amid audit of its AI algorithms. Retrieved from https://fortune.com/2021/01/19/hirevue-drops-facial-monitoring-amid-a-i-algorithm-audit/

Kawakami, K., Dovidio, J. F., & van Kamp, S. (2005). Kicking the habit: Effects of nonstereotypic association training and correction processes on hiring decisions. *Journal of Experimental Social Psychology*, *41*(1), 68–75. doi:10.1016/J.JESP.2004.05.004

Kawakami, K., Dovidio, J. F., & van Kamp, S. (2007). The impact of counterstereotypic training and related correction processes on the application of stereotypes. *Group Processes & Intergroup Relations*, *10*(2), 139–156. doi:10.1177/1368430207074725

Kern, M. L., Eichstaedt, J. C., Schwartz, H. A., Dziurzynski, L., Ungar, L. H., Stillwell, D. J., ... Seligman, M. E. P. (2014). The online social self: An open vocabulary approach to personality. *Assessment*, *21*(2), 158–169. doi:10.1177/1073191113514104

Köchling, A., Riazy, S., Wehner, M. C., & Simbeck, K. (2021). Highly accurate, but still discriminatory: A Fairness evaluation of algorithmic video analysis in the recruitment context. *Business and Information Systems Engineering*, *63*(1), 39–54. doi:10.1007/s12599-020-00673-w

Kuncel, N. R., Ones, D. S., & Sackett, P. R. (2010). Individual differences as predictors of work, educational, and broad life outcomes. *Personality and Individual Differences*, *49*(4), 331–336. doi:10.1016/j.paid.2010.03.042

Kwon, S., Yeon Choeh, J., & Lee, J. W. (2013). User-personality classification based on the non-verbal cues from spoken conversations. *International Journal of Computational Intelligence Systems*, *6*(4), 739–749. doi:10.1080/18756891.2013.804143

Lambiotte, R., & Kosinski, M. (2014). Tracking the digital footprints of personality. *Proceedings of the IEEE*, *102*(12), 1934–1939. doi:10.1109/JPROC.2014.2359054

Levashina, J., Hartwell, C. J., Morgeson, F. P., & Campion, M. A. (2014). The structured employment interview: Narrative and quantitative review of the research literature. *Personnel Psychology*, *67*(1), 241–293. doi:10.1111/peps.12052

Liu, W., Bartkoski, T. J., Brandt, O. S., Theys, E. R., & Lobbe, C. E. (2021). Poster presented at the Society of Industry and Organisational Psychology Annual Conference.

Loper, E., & Bird, S. (2002, May 17). *NLTK: The Natural Language Toolkit*. Retrieved from https://arxiv.org/abs/cs/0205028v1

Macan, T. (2009). The employment interview: A review of current studies and directions for future research. *Human Resource Management Review*, *19*(3), 203–218. doi:10.1016/J.HRMR.2009.03.006

Malta, AI (2019). Towards ethical and trustworthy AI. Retrieved from https://malta.ai/wp-content/uploads/2019/10/Malta_Towards_Ethical_and_Trustworthy_AI_vFINAL.pdf

Maltby, J., Day, L., & Macaskill, A. (2017). *Personality, individual differences and intelligence* (4th ed.). Pearson.

Mason, J. S., & Thompson, J. (1993). Gender effects in speaker recognition. *ICSP*, 733–736. Retrieved from https://pdfs.semanticscholar.org/3078/5e7e6a27995f5fd85365f707634f9bdbdc1b.pdf

Mccarthy, J. M., Van Iddekinge, C. H., & Campion, M. A. (2010). Are highly structured job interviews resistant to demographic similarity effects? *Personnel Psychology*, *63*(2), 325–359. doi:10.1111/j.1744-6570.2010.01172.x

McDaniel, M. A., Whetzel, D. L., Schmidt, F. L., & Maurer, S. D. (1994). The validity of employment interviews: A comprehensive review and meta-analysis. *Journal of Applied Psychology*, *79*(4), 599–616. doi:10.1037/0021-9010.79.4.599

Mohammadi, G., Origlia, A., Filippone, M., & Vinciarelli, A. (2012). From speech to personality: Mapping voice quality and intonation into personality differences. In Proceedings of the 20th ACM International Conference on Multimedia (pp. 789–792). doi:10.1145/2393347.2396313

Mohammadi, G., & Vinciarelli, A. (2012). Automatic personality perception: Prediction of trait attribution based on prosodic features. *IEEE Transactions on Affective Computing*, *3*(3), 273–284. doi:10.1109/T-AFFC.2012.5

Nguyen, L. S., Frauendorfer, D., Mast, M. S., & Gatica-Perez, D. (2014). Hire me: Computational inference of hirability in employment interviews based on nonverbal behavior. *IEEE Transactions on Multimedia*, *16*(4), 1018–1031. doi:10.1109/TMM.2014.2307169

Nguyen, L. S., & Gatica-Perez, D. (2015). I would hire you in a minute. In Proceedings of the 2015 ACM on International Conference on Multimodal Interaction (pp. 51–58). doi:10.1145/2818346.2820760

Nguyen, L. S., & Gatica-Perez, D. (2016). Hirability in the wild: Analysis of online conversational video resumes. *IEEE Transactions on Multimedia*, *18*(7), 1422–1437. doi:10.1109/TMM.2016.2557058

Palanica, A., Thommandram, A., Lee, A., Li, M., & Fossat, Y. (2019). Do you understand the words that are comin outta my mouth? Voice assistant comprehension of medication names. *Npj Digital Medicine*, *2*(1), 1–6. doi:10.1038/s41746-019-0133-x

Park, G., Andrew Schwartz, H., Eichstaedt, J. C., Kern, M. L., Kosinski, M., Stillwell, D. J., ... Seligman, M. E. P. (2015). Automatic personality assessment through social media language. *Journal of Personality and Social Psychology*, *108*(6), 934–952. doi:10.1037/pspp0000020

Pennebaker, J. W., Boyd, R. L., Jordan, K., & Blackburn, K. (2015). The development and psychometric properties of LIWC2015. Retrieved from https://repositories.lib.utexas.edu/handle/2152/31333

Pennebaker, J. W., & King, L. A. (1999). Linguistic styles: Language use as an individual difference. *Journal of Personality and Social Psychology*, *77*(6), 1296–1312. doi:10.1037/0022-3514.77.6.1296

Prendergast, C., & Topel, R. (1993). Discretion and bias in performance evaluation. *European Economic Review*, *37*(2–3), 355–365. doi:10.1016/0014-2921(93)90024-5

Raghavan, M., & Barocas, S. (2019). Challenges for mitigating bias in algorithmic hiring. Retrieved from https://www.brookings.edu/research/challenges-for-mitigating-bias-in-algorithmic-hiring/

Rasmussen, K. G. (1984). Nonverbal behavior, verbal behavior, resumé credentials, and selection interview outcomes. *Journal of Applied Psychology*, *69*(4), 551–556. doi:10.1037/0021-9010.69.4.551

Risavy, S. D., & Hausdorf, P. A. (2011). Personality testing in personnel selection: Adverse impact and differential hiring rates. *International Journal of Selection and Assessment*, *19*(1), 18–30. doi:10.1111/j.1468-2389.2011.00531.x

Rupasinghe, A. T., Gunawardena, N. L., Shujan, S., & Atukorale, D. A. S. (2017). Scaling personality traits of interviewees in an online job interview by vocal spectrum and facial cue analysis. In 16th International Conference on Advances in ICT for Emerging Regions (pp. 288–295). doi:10.1109/ICTER.2016.7829933

Sarkar, C., Bhatia, S., Agarwal, A., & Li, J. (2014). Feature analysis for computational personality recognition using YouTube personality data set. In Proceedings of the 2014 Workshop on Computational Personality Recognition (pp. 11–14). doi:10.1145/2659522.2659528

Schawbel, D. (2020). How coronavirus is accelerating remote job searching, interviewing and hiring. Retrieved from https://www.linkedin.com/pulse/how-coronavirus-accelerating-remote-job-searching-hiring-dan-schawbel

Schmidt, F. L., & Hunter, J. E. (1998). The validity and utility of selection methods in personnel psychology: Practical and theoretical implications of 85 years of research findings. *Psychological Bulletin*, *124*(2), 262–274. doi:10.1037/0033-2909.124.2.262

Schmidt, F. L., Oh, I.-S., & Shaffer, J. A. (2016). The validity and utility of selection methods in personnel psychology: Practical and theoretical Implications of 100 Years. doi:10.13140/RG.2.2.18843.26400

Schmitt, N. (2014). Personality and cognitive ability as predictors of effective performance at work. *Annual Review of Organizational Psychology and Organizational Behavior*, *1*(1), 45–65. doi:10.1146/annurev-orgpsych-031413-091255

Schwartz, H. A., Eichstaedt, J. C., Kern, M. L., Dziurzynski, L., Ramones, S. M., Agrawal, M., … Ungar, L. H. (2013). Personality, gender, and age in the language of social media: The open-vocabulary approach. *PLoS ONE*, *8*(9), e73791. doi:10.1371/journal.pone.0073791

Singh, S., Darwish, T. K., & Potočnik, K. (2016). Measuring organizational performance: A case for subjective measures. *British Journal of Management*, 27(1), 214–224. doi: 10.1111/1467-8551.12126

Society for Industrial and Organizational Psychology. (2018). *Psychology's guidelines for education and training 2018* (5th ed.). Retrieved from https://www.apa.org/ed/acc reditation/about/policies/personnel-selection-procedures.pdf

Stone, P. J., Dunphi, D., Marshall, S. S., & Olgilvie, D. M. (1966). *The general inquirer: A computer approach to content analysis*. MIT Press.

Suen, H.-Y., Hung, K.-E., & Lin, C.-L. (2019). TensorFlow-based automatic personality recognition used in asynchronous video interviews. *IEEE Access*, 7, 61018–61023. doi:10.1109/ACCESS.2019.2902863

Tatman, R. (2017). Gender and dialect bias in YouTube's automatic captions. In Proceedings of the First ACL Workshop on Ethics in Natural Language Processing (pp. 53–59). doi:10.18653/v1/W17-1606

Tatman, R., & Kasten, C. (2017). Effects of talker dialect, gender & race on accuracy of bing speech and youtube automatic captions. In Proceedings of the Annual Conference of the International Speech Communication Association, 2017-Augus (pp. 934–938). INTERSPEECH. doi:10. 21437/Interspeech.2017-1746

The Predictive Index. (2020). The guide to structured interviews: The 7 steps to implementing a better interviewing process at your company. Retrieved from https://www.predictive success.com/wp-content/uploads/2020/03/GuideStructuredI nterview.pdf

Tian, Y. L., Kanade, T., & Conn, J. F. (2001). Recognizing action units for facial expression analysis. *IEEE Transactions on Pattern Analysis and Machine Intelligence*, 23(2), 97–115. doi:10.1109/34.908962

Vrij, A., Dragt, A., & Koppelaar, L. (1992). Interviews with ethnic interviewees: Non-verbal communication errors in impression formation. *Journal of Community & Applied Social Psychology*, 2(3), 199–208. doi:10.1002/CASP.2450020304

Wiesner, W. H., & Cronshaw, S. F. (1988). A meta-analytic investigation of the impact of interview format and degree of structure on the validity of the employment interview. *Journal of Occupational Psychology*, 61(4), 275–290. doi:10.1111/j.2044-8325.1988.tb00467.x

Wilson, J. H., & Daugherty, P. R. (2018). Collaborative intelligence: Humans and AI are joining forces. *Harvard Business Review*. Retrieved from https://hbr.org/2018/07/collaborative-intelligence-humans-and-ai-are-joining-forces

Yarkoni, T. (2010). Personality in 100,000 words: A large-scale analysis of personality and word use among bloggers. *Journal of Research in Personality*, 44(3), 363–373. doi:10.1016/j.jrp.2010.04.001

Youyou, W., Kosinski, M., & Stillwell, D. (2015). Computer-based personality judgments are more accurate than those made by humans. *Proceedings of the National Academy of Sciences*, 112(4), 1036–1040. doi:10.1073/PNAS.1418680112

4

MINING DIGITAL TALENT SIGNALS

What do you think tells or reveals the most about you, your carefully curated resumé, or your social media feed? I think we all would agree that the latter would give any stranger an accurate picture of your unique characteristics, life history, and talents. If I know that you spend a lot of time browsing and contributing to Wikipedia, as opposed to if I know you spend your time bouncing from one influencer to the next on YouTube, I can make a safe bet that you're intellectually curious.

It is no longer insightful or profound to say that the things we consume, create, and engage with online are accurate representations of our identity. In fact, scientists have long known that there is a strong relationship between our identity and consumer behavior; the things we buy, places we visit, and how we decorate our homes reveal a remarkable amount about us (Gosling, Ko, Mannarelli, & Morris, 2002; Kim & Song, 2014; Sandy, Gosling, & Durant, 2013). As connected technologies continue to become deeply integrated into our lives, the same is true for our online behavior (Kosinski, Stillwell, & Graepel, 2013).

Advancements in technology and digital services present significant opportunities to change the way we select and identity talent. If each person is generating a sea of data each day, revealing accurate and objective signals into their behavior, skills, and values, the idea of having to physically take an assessment starts to look antiqued. We already know that resumes are faked (Turczynski, 2021), interviews are biased (Derous, Buijsrogge, Roulin, & Duyck, 2016), and there is an inequality in access to hiring opportunities (Bjerk, 2008; Clayton, Williams, & Howell, 2014), so a strong case can be made for mining applicants' online behavior for digital talent signals to overcome these issues and usher in more effective and equitable selection practices. The goal of this chapter is to convince you that this is possible, and not just another way for tech platforms and organizations to continue eroding our privacy.

This chapter is organized around three themes. The first is to explore the extent to which the theory of talent signals, as introduced in chapter 2, is actually supported by empirical evidence. Here, we will summarize the scientific literature that has used vast amounts of data and artificial intelligence (AI) to demonstrate that mining our digital footprints can yield unique insights into us. The second is to explore the practical applications of these next gen assessments. Specifically, how can digital signals be used by organizations in the war for talent, and how can job seekers use their digital footprint to open up new career opportunities? Finally, we outline the key ethical considerations and obstacles that must be addressed before such technology can be applied to one's ability to gain meaningful employment.

At the end of this chapter, you will be able to answer the following questions:

1. How do digital footprints compare to existing assessment data?

2. What can our social media, browsing history, and meta-data tell us about our personality?

3. To what extent can digital forms of language inform talent profiles?

4. How could I use digital footprints in my selection practices?

5. What are the risks and ethical concerns when using this type of data?

YOU ARE WHAT YOU LIKE

Beyond measuring one's technical ability, the fundamental objective of all talent assessments is to sufficiently understand one's tendency to behave in a given way and infer that they will continue to do so in the future. If talent is the product of the right personality in the right place (Chamorro-Premuzic, Winsborough, Sherman, & Hogan, 2016), recruiters need more accurate and comprehensive tools of one's dispositions, decision-making styles, and motivations. We attempt to infer these things through interviews and by studying one's career history, deducing what tasks they are skilled at or their approach to communicating and working with others. While psychometric surveys can do this in a more standardized and transparent way, these traditional approaches are flawed in four ways: (1) They mostly rely on expert raters, which can be prone to bias (Purkiss, Perrewé, Gillespie, Mayes, & Ferris, 2006). (2) They can easily be faked, gamed, or cheated (Melchers, Roulin, & Buehl, 2020; Ones & Viswesvaran, 1998). (3) They rely mostly on subjective or quasi-objective data sampled at one point in time which could be affected by external factors (Ahuja & Arora, 2017). (4) High volumes and the need for scale typically bottleneck the "best in class" applications of these methodologies (Forbes Human Resources Council, 2017). Mining our digital footprints, specifically, our social media profiles, offers a powerful alternative to these practices.

Analyzing and interpreting one's online and social media history has long been of interest to recruiters and psychologists alike. The ability to quickly search for an individual and learn how they present themselves, their interests, and professional experience is intuitively useful and insightful. Yet we use these sources of information in a clumsy way that only serves to repeat the many mistakes and flaws of human judgment that we experience in traditional assessment contexts. AI offers a solution here. By mining one's online behavior at a granular level, taking into account every click, message, and endorsement one makes, we can generate an empirical and reliable assessment of one's talents. For comparison, a structured interview or personality survey asks users questions about how one would behave. These answers are then interpreted and then used to score one's talent potential. AI algorithms that were developed to use our digital footprints can replicate this process at greater volumes, across multiple contexts, and process infinitely more pieces of data that a human could make sense of.

To some, this may sound scary, to others, claims about AI's ability to understand humans are overhyped. Yet, there is a well-established body of scientific literature that provides sufficient support for the theory of talent signals, and that our online history, social media, and metadata, if used properly, offer powerful insights for recruiters. Put another way, we are what we like.

The relationship between online behavior and psychological variables has been a hot topic since the advent of "Web

2.0" in the late 1990s, with many exploring how our identities are expressed online (Anderson, Fagan, Woodnutt, & Chamorro-Premuzic, 2012). Most of this research, however, was still conducted using survey methodologies, meaning its insights were restricted and subject to the many limitations that often plague much psychological research (i.e., self-report methods, small WEIRD samples; Rad, Martingano, & Ginges, 2018). However, as social media platforms like Facebook become ubiquitous with the internet (acquiring nearly three billion monthly users) and the ability to scrape and analyze data from these platforms became easy, a new program of research begun, led by Prof. Michal Kosinski and Prof. David Stillwell at Cambridge University.

In now a seminal study, Kosinski et al. (2013) sought to demonstrate how publicly accessible digital footprints left on social media sites can accurately predict private attributes such as our demographics, values, personality, and intelligence. To answer this question, they recruited over 58,000 people who completed a battery of psychometric surveys and gathered over 10 million digital records, specifically their Facebook likes. In line with the theory of talent signals, they postulated that when aggregated, the pages an individual likes on Facebook reveal an accurate portrayal of their psychological profile. Their AI algorithms found this to be true.

First, they sought to predict one's demographic factors. They found that one's age and gender could be detected with 75%–95% accuracy. Second, they found Facebook likes to be moderately correlated with one's intelligence ($r = 0.39$). Finally, one's personality could also be accurately detected, with correlations ranging between 0.29 (conscientiousness) and 0.43 (openness to experience). These findings are noteworthy as they demonstrate that a single type of digital footprint can accurately predict psychological characteristics that have been consistently demonstrated to influence job performance and potential (Chamorro-Premuzic & Furnham, 2010).

In a follow-up study, the same team of researchers sought to compare how accurate their social media algorithms were compared to one's colleagues, friends, and families (Youyou, Kosinski, & Stillwell, 2015). To much surprise, they not only found that one's digital footprints provide more accurate evaluations of one's personality than their colleagues and family members but also the amount of data needed to achieve such accuracy was shockingly small. For example, the average correlation between self-evaluations of personality and those of a work colleague is 0.27. With only 10 Facebook likes, their algorithm could surpass this. With 100 likes, the algorithm could surpass the evaluations of one's closest friends or housemates ($r = 0.45$). With 150 likes, the evaluations of one's closest family members ($r = 0.50$) were surpassed, and with 300 likes, the algorithm could match the evaluations of one's spouse ($r = 0.58$). Furthermore, their algorithm could also predict an individual's values (the precursor for culture fit; Hogan & Bond, 2009) better than human raters. These findings demonstrate that an algorithm trained upon a single source of seemingly unobtrusive and irrelevant source of behavioral data can reveal more accurate insights about one's decision-making, problem-solving, and relational tendencies than the countless life experiences and intimacies acquired by our nearest and dearest.

One criticism of the aforementioned research is that it is based on one source and type of digital record, the Facebook like. Can other platforms and record types be just as revealing? Guntuku et al. (2017) addressed this question and sought to investigate whether the images one posts and endorses on sites such as Twitter reveal one's personality. Similar to Kosinski et al. (2013), they found that an image's composition (i.e. brightness, saturation, and hue) and subject was correlated with one's Big Five personality profile. Similar findings can also be found across other platforms, including Spotify listening history (Anderson et al., 2021), Goodreads book preferences (Annalyn, Bos, Sigal, & Li, 2020), and smartphone sensors and activity (de Montjoye, Quoidbach, Robic, & Pentland, 2013; Stachl et al., 2020). Furthermore, our digital records can predict more than just our personality. Studies have found social media records to predict income (Matz, Menges, Stillwell, & Schwartz, 2019) and occupational status (Preoţiuc-Pietro, Lampos, & Aletras, 2015), alongside career preferences and vocational interests (Kern, McCarthy, Chakrabarty, & Rizoiu, 2019).

Summarizing this body of research, Azucar, Marengo, and Settanni (2018) conducted a meta-analysis of 14 separate studies containing different types of social media records from a variety of platforms in an attempt to estimate the true prediction of one's personality. Through this process, they arrived at a number of conclusions. First, the correlation between digital footprints acquired through social media, and personality ranges between 0.29 and 0.40 (agreeableness and extraversion, respectively). This moderate and reliable effect size is what is commonly found when studying the relationship between personality and observed behaviors, such as job performance (Chamorro-Premuzic & Furnham, 2010). Second, the accuracy of predictions increases when more than one type of digital footprint is used. This finding is intuitive and is analogous with well-designed assessment procedures whereby a recruiter will gather evaluations from a variety of sources using a variety of methods (i.e. peer ratings, job simulations, assessment surveys, etc.). Accordingly, digital footprint-powered talent assessments should incorporate a variety of sources to increase both the reliability and validity of its talent evaluations.

Much of the reviewed research has focused on the prediction of personality. While we acknowledge one's ability to perform in a given role is the result of technical, social, and motivational factors, the emphasis on these new method-ology's ability to predict personality is noteworthy as it has been shown to be a valid and stable predictor of performance across industries, job levels, and cultures (Barrick & Mount, 1991; Kuncel, Ones, & Sackett, 2010; Rothmann & Coetzer, 2003; Schmidt & Hunter, 1998; Schmitt, 2014). From a practical perspective, it is easy to see how these findings could be applied. Rather than request an individual to complete a long and expensive psychometric survey, a secure and private web application would allow applicants to donate their social media data, allowing an algorithm to objectively evaluate their talents in microseconds. Such a process would be cheap, require no time investment from the applicant, and allow the recruiter to expand its hiring pool. The adoption of such tools would have the added benefit of increasing HR practitioners use of scientific concepts and constructs in their talent prac-tices, moving away from gut instinct or intuitive evaluations of one's potential, and enabling organizations to start to leverage 50 years of research that has demonstrated the importance of the personality in the workplace, such as pre-dicting engagement, burnout, and counterproductive or toxic behaviors (Alarcon, Eschleman, & Bowling, 2009; Berry, Ones, & Sackett, 2007; Jensen & Patel, 2011; Shukla, Adhikari, & Singh, 2015; Swider & Zimmerman, 2010; Young, Glerum, Wang, & Joseph, 2018).

NATURAL LANGUAGE PROCESSING AND TALENT SIGNALS

Another type of digital record that has been shown to have high validity and many practical applications is language. Specifically, the language we use across digital forms of communication such as email, SMS, and social media. Psychologists have long studied the relationship between language, originating from Freud's psychoanalytic methodologies to more modern approaches that have sought to connect the frequency and style of language to understanding how people think, act, and make decisions (Allport & Odbert, 1936). After all, language is the only way we can truly understand how people describe themselves, others, and the world (Tausczik & Pennebaker, 2010). With the rise of digital communication, computational methods, and the prevalence of computer-mediated communication via email, Slack, and WhatsApp (a trend that will not be slowing down thanks to the COVID-19 pandemic), natural language processing (NLP) has become a lively field of study with increasingly commercial applications. Unlike other digital records that can only be recorded or interpreted within the context of a single platform (i.e. Facebook likes), language is platform-neutral, highly interpretable, and a rich source of easily accessible and relevant data.

AI works to turn language into quantifiable talent signals by building large dictionaries of words and phrases, which are then grouped together by semantic themes or grammatical classifications. Once this lexicon has been developed, algorithms can then be tuned to identify trends that people are discussing (widely used in organizational culture and employee engagement contexts), identify keywords related to career history, technical abilities, and prior experience (useful to automate the screening of resumes and job applications), or how the use of specific words and themes are related to different work-related behaviors and outcomes.

Resume Screening

It is estimated that each corporate job offer attracts 250 resumes and that hiring managers will typically spend less than six minutes reviewing a CV before making rejecting a candidate (CareerBuilder, 2014). These statistics reveal how inefficient and unfair the resume is. Applicants will spend hours crafting their resume, only for a hiring manager to screen it out based on arbitrary attributes, heuristics, or at worst, biases (Derous & Ryan, 2019). For example, seminal studies have shown that when names or other gender and ethnicity variables are blinded or removed from resumes, there is a significant increase in minority groups being selected for the next phase in the hiring process (Joseph, 2016).

The use of AI algorithms to process and screen resumes has been a hot topic of research and practice, and we envision it to continue to grow. There are three key advantages of using AI to screen resumes. First, algorithms can detect keywords and phrases that have been empirically keyed against past performance, enabling an objective and data-driven decision criteria (Sajjadiani, Sojourner, Kammeyer-Mueller, & Mykerezi, 2019). Second, gender, age, and ethnicity bias can be more readily detected and controlled, unlike human raters (Deshpande, Pan, & Foulds, 2020). Last, recruiter's time is freed up, enabling them to spend more time engaging the most promising candidates. Companies using resume parsing tools such as Textio and Textkernel report to be identifying high-quality applicants and reducing the "time to fill" (Coughlin, 2018; Textkernel, 2021).

Culture Fit and Employee Engagement

Organizations are increasingly hiring for culture fit, ensuring that their employees' values are closely aligned with those of the organization (Dvorak & Pendell, 2018). Similarly, leaders continue to invest great resources into measuring and tracking their employees' engagement. These are laudable endeavors as improving culture fit and engagement is related to employee well-being, job satisfaction, and performance (De Cooman et al., 2009; Kristof, 1996; Saks, 2006; Westerman & Cyr, 2004). Can NLP provide leaders with greater insight into their employees?

First, NLP models have been developed to measure various dimensions of organizational culture and predict firm performance (Mayew & Venkatachalam, 2012; Pandey & Pandey, 2019). Second, internal and external sources of text data can be used to accurately infer employees' level of engagement (Golestani et al., 2018; Shami, Muller, Pal, Masli, & Geyer, 2015). Third, crowdsourced review sites such as Glassdoor have been found to predict employee sentiment and satisfaction (Landers, Brusso, & Auer, 2019). Companies such as CultureAmp and CultureX have already commercialized these findings, enabling leaders to utilize the plethora of communication data sitting on their company's servers.

Talent Assessment

Can NLP methods replace the need to complete long psychometric surveys? The research suggests, yes! A seminal study by Park et al. (2015) sought to train machine-learning algorithms to measure and detect personality profiles using the language used online. Gathering historical status updates from over 60,000 Facebook users, they were able to accurately predict Big Five personality profiles (correlations ranging between 0.35 and 0.43). Moreover, these language-based models were found to have a high degree of convergence with human raters and were highly stable over a six-month period.

In 2018, we extended this research to explore the extent to which toxic and maladaptive personalities could also be predicted (Akhtar, Winsborough, Ort, Johnson, & Chamorro-Premuzic, 2018). We found that "dark side" traits that contribute toward leadership ineffectiveness, overconfidence, and dysfunctional culture could be detected using one's status updates, albeit less so ($r = 0.08$ to 0.27). For instance, individuals who were rated as overconfident, narcissistic, status-obsessed, and manipulative were more likely to use language that contained references to achievements, power, and themselves. Similarly, individuals who are emotionally volatile, moody, and temperamental were more likely to use language that was negative in its sentiment and describe fewer positive emotions.

Beyond personality, other researchers have found online language to also predict work-relevant characteristics. Specifically, one's values, vocational preferences, and emotional resilience (Boyd et al., 2015; Kern et al., 2019; Pang et al., 2020; Schwartz et al., 2013; Sun, Schwartz, Son, Kern, & Vazire, 2020).

USES AND APPLICATIONS

In the near future, we envision digital records becoming commonplace in the recruitment process. The reviewed research demonstrates their ability to accurately measure relevant talents and characteristics, and evidence suggests that as more and diverse digital records can be aggregated and analyzed, the accuracy of this prediction will only increase (Azucar et al., 2018). While there are technological and ethical considerations to contend with, we do see five practical applications for this new methodology.

Prehire Assessments

For many corporate positions, it is not uncommon to require applicants to first complete a battery of assessments, typically measuring personality and cognitive ability. The results of which are used to "screen out" the first tranche of applicants who do not meet specified criteria. Unfortunately, this results in a lot of wasted time and effort from job seekers who repeat the process until they find employment. For recruiters, using traditional prehire assessments slows down the process and results in a longer time to fill (Sambandam, 2019). Using digital records could sufficiently speed up the process without a loss of accuracy. For instance, we imagine a "one-click" assessment whereby an applicant donates their digital records and is then profiled by an AI algorithm, revealing their personality, values, career history, and interests. This would not only allow applicants to effortlessly apply for many jobs, but recruiters would also be rewarded with a more holistic and accurate insight into one's talents, enabling them to better assess suitability and fit for the role. Social media is already factored into the hiring process; we should work to use these data in a fairer, more organized, and scientific manner (Davison, Bing, Kluemper, & Roth, 2016).

Improving Diversity and Culture Fit

Robust hiring practices are a critical way for organizations to create more diverse, inclusive, and equitable workplaces (Woods & Tharakan, 2021). In fact, research demonstrates scientific assessments that minimize human judgments and subjectivity are one of the most effective ways to make fairer hiring decisions (Trindel, Polli, & Glazebrook, 2020). In line with this, the use of digital records offers an exciting next step in this endeavor. As argued above, digital records not only lower the barrier to entry (a significant issue when recruiting from underserved communities; De Haan, 2018) but also recruiters would be able to source talent from larger and diverse pools (Ajunwa & Schlund, 2020). In addition, recruiters can use such tools to improve job and culture fit. Studies have already shown that digital records can predict our cultural preferences and vocational interests (Boyd et al., 2015; Kern et al., 2019). Automatically profiling candidates on these dimensions can be used by recruiters to place people in roles that they will find intrinsically motivating and engaging, improving job performance and lowering turnover (Nucleus Research, 2021).

Internal Talent Assessment and Analytics

The research reviewed has largely focused on an individual's social media data. Although we do believe that this is a useful source of data, it is important to consider the fundamental principle behind these findings – disparate and unexpected digital records of behavior reveal meaningful psychological insights. This means that organizations can leverage this principle to drastically change the way it manages internal talent assessments and analytics. Collating records across Slack, calendar invites, and other internal platforms would reveal how people get work done and what talents are needed to thrive. There are already many vendors offering organizations tools to leverage these internal digital records (i.e., CultureAmp, Glint, Microsoft, Glikon, etc.). Collecting accurate and scientific talent data to improve internal hiring decisions and succession planning is difficult due to survey fatigue, disorganized practices, and office politics (Maurer, 2015). However, an organization's workforce generates vast swathes of behavioral data, and if collected and organized carefully, this would negate these limitations and enable more data-driven talent practices.

Automated Coaching and Development

It is estimated that only 10% of people are truly self-aware at work (Eurich, 2018) and that 70% of an organization's top talent leave because they are not given the development opportunities to achieve their professional goals (CEB, 2015). Couple these statistics with the fact that we are living in a crisis of misunderstanding whereby managers and leaders can't engage their teams (Mann & Harter, 2016) and communicating and collaborating with our colleagues continues to be a leading source of frustration and ineffectiveness (Allen, Yoerger, Lehmann-Willenbrock, & Jones, 2015), it is easy to make the case that leaders need to provide their employees with more feedback and coaching. Attempting to fix these issues are companies such as BetterUp, Ezra, and Deeper Signals, who are working to provide more data-driven coaching to employees. However, borrowing from the wearables industry, in the near future, we see an opportunity to source digital records and powering on-demand and automated feedback, helping employees understand their mood, reputation and well-being, and serving practical advice and recommendations (The School of Life, 2016). This approach would remove the need for costly assessments and executive coaches, and instead provide real-time nudging based on thousands of personal data points, helping people work to their full potential.

Talent Passports

The gig economy has enabled many to eschew traditional forms of employment. Powered by platforms such as Upwork and Fiverr, skilled professionals can be easy connected with people who need and are willing to pay for their expertise.

Concurrently, we see the continued growth of blockchain technologies where its digital ledgers track previous transactions, ownership, and contracts. Connecting these socio-technological trends with the research reviewed in this chapter, we foresee a future whereby "talent passports" become an influential part of the hiring process. The talent passport would contain a digital ledger of one's career history, educational and professional achievements, alongside their hard and soft talents. The advantage of the talent passport is threefold. First, it would drastically disrupt and negate much of the current recruitment process. Applicants would be able to instantly share their entire experience and talents, and recruiters would not need to subject the applicant to more assessments or poorly structured interviews. Second, it would allow individuals to present themselves to their fullest and be objectively assessed on their talents, bringing more objectivity and fairness to the process. Last, it would allow those who prefer more fluid forms of employment to easily move from one employer to the next as the talent passport would be standardized and recognized across industries – just like travel passports!

THE DIGITAL PANOPTICON: ETHICAL RISKS AND LIMITATIONS

It is easy to flag the ethical risks and limitations associated with the use of digital records. In a world that is increasingly surveilled and the presence of legitimate concerns that algorithms are increasingly weaponized to work against our freedoms and self-interest is growing, the idea of tying our employment to more digital records that we may not even be conscious of is dangerous. We have seen, through the Cambridge Analytica scandal, that our digital records can be turned into psychological indicators that are used to push political messaging (Matz, Kosinski, Nave, & Stillwell, 2017; Nature, 2018), that digital records can be used to accurately identify our sexuality (Wang & Kosinski, 2018), and they can work against ideals of fairer and less biased hiring practices (i.e., Amazon's sexist resumé parser; Dastin, 2018). While there is clear cause for caution, these challenges are not insurmountable.

As Cathy O'Neil highlights, algorithms that process vast and disparate amounts of data, without little oversight can quickly become weapons of math destruction (O'Neil, 2016). We believe it is better to be proactive about the future and how this technology develops, otherwise the use of such data will be transformed into a digital panopticon whereby employers can surveil their applicants and harm their ability to find employment. It is, therefore, critical that developers and vendors of these next gen assessments think critically and intentionally about the following questions (Yam & Skorburg, 2021):

1. *A lack of transparency*: To what extent do applicants and recruiters know how their data are being processed, weighted, and analyzed by the algorithm?

2. *Power asymmetry*: What can be done to equalize the imbalance of power between those wielding the algorithm and those being subjected to its decisions?

3. *Bias and discrimination*: Can the developers and users of talent algorithms demonstrate that there is no adverse impact on the selection of minority and protected groups?

4. *Privacy*: Are the requested digital records relevant, made clear to the applicant, and what safeguards are being made to ensure their privacy is being protected?

Addressing such questions not only requires an interdisciplinary approach, ranging across psychologists, computer scientists, and civil rights experts but also requires a fundamental shift in how many of us engage with technology and our relationship with data. Specifically, we must not allow a handful of technology companies to have a monopoly on our digital records and online identity. While some of the "FAANG" companies are starting to address this issue, the promise and opportunity to be gained by applicants and recruiters in using digital records cannot be fully realized until individuals can easily access their digital records and have the power to choose what can and cannot be shared with employers and organizations. Meanwhile, researchers and scientists must continue to research ways to detect and limit algorithmic bias and continue to prove the validity of digital records in the prediction of job performance and career success. The cost of not pushing for these changes will at best be that the dysfunctional hiring practices that are currently used will persist, or at worst will violate our privacy and right to work.

REFERENCES

Ahuja, T., & Arora, D. (2017). Understanding interviewee behavior and factors affecting performance in interview. *International Journal of Innovation and Research in Educational Sciences*, 4(3), 302–305. http://ijires.org/administrator/components/com_jresearch/files/publications/IJIRES_910__FINAL.pdf

Ajunwa, I., & Schlund, R. (2020). Algorithms and the social organization of work. In M. D. Dubber, F. Pasquale, & S. Das (Eds.), *The Oxford handbook of ethics of AI* (pp.

803–822). Oxford University Press. doi:10.1093/oxfordhb/9780190067397.013.52

Akhtar, R., Winsborough, D., Ort, U., Johnson, A., & Chamorro-Premuzic, T. (2018). Detecting the dark side of personality using social media status updates. *Personality and Individual Differences*, *132*, 90–97. doi:10.1016/J.PAID.2018.05.026

Alarcon, G., Eschleman, K. J., & Bowling, N. A. (2009). Relationships between personality variables and burnout: A meta-analysis. *Work & Stress*, *23*(3), 244–263. doi:10.1080/02678370903282600

Allen, J. A., Yoerger, M. A., Lehmann-Willenbrock, N., & Jones, J. (2015). Would you please stop that!?: The relationship between counterproductive meeting behaviors, employee voice, and trust. *The Journal of Management Development*, *34*(10), 1272–1287. doi:10.1108/JMD-02-2015-0032

Allport, G. W., & Odbert, H. S. (1936). Trait-names: A psycho-lexical study. *Psychological Monographs*, *47*(1), i–171. doi:10.1037/h0093360

Anderson, B., Fagan, P., Woodnutt, T., & Chamorro-Premuzic, T. (2012). Facebook psychology: Popular questions answered by research. *Psychology of Popular Media Culture*, *1*(1), 23–37. doi:10.1037/a0026452

Anderson, I., Gil, S., Gibson, C., Wolf, S., Shapiro, W., Semerci, O., & Greenberg, D. M. (2021). "Just the Way You Are": Linking music listening on Spotify and personality. *Social Psychological and Personality Science*, *12*(4), 561–572. doi:10.1177/1948550620923228

Annalyn, N., Bos, M. W., Sigal, L., & Li, B. (2020). Predicting personality from book preferences with user-generated content labels. *IEEE Transactions on Affective Computing*, *11*(3), 482–492. doi:10.1109/TAFFC.2018.2808349

Azucar, D., Marengo, D., & Settanni, M. (2018). Predicting the Big 5 personality traits from digital footprints on social media: A meta-analysis. *Personality and Individual Differences*, *124*, 150–159. doi:10.1016/j.paid.2017.12.018

Barrick, M. R., & Mount, M. K. (1991). The Big five personality dimensions and job performance: A meta-analysis. *Personnel Psychology*, *44*(1), 1–26. doi:10.1111/j.1744-6570.1991.tb00688.x

Berry, C. M., Ones, D. S., & Sackett, P. R. (2007). Interpersonal deviance, organizational deviance, and their common correlates: A review and meta-analysis. *Journal of Applied Psychology*, *92*(2), 410–424. doi:10.1037/0021-9010.92.2.410

Bjerk, D. (2008). Glass ceilings or sticky floors? Statistical discrimination in a dynamic model of hiring and promotion. *Economic Journal*, *118*(530), 961–982. doi:10.1111/j.1468-0297.2008.02157.x

Boyd, R. L., Wilson, S. R., Pennebaker, J. W., Kosinski, M., Stillwell, D. J., & Mihalcea, R. (2015). Values in words: Using language to evaluate and understand personal values. *Proceedings of the 9th International Conference on Web and Social Media*, *9*(1), 31–40. Retrieved from https://ojs.aaai.org/index.php/ICWSM/article/view/14589

CareerBuilder. (2014). Hiring managers rank best and worst words to use in a resume in new CareerBuilder survey. Retrieved from http://press.careerbuilder.com/2014-03-13-Hiring-Managers-Rank-Best-and-Worst-Words-to-Use-in-a-Resume-in-New-CareerBuilder-Survey

CEB. (2015). Seventy percent of employees unhappy with career opportunities. Retrieved from https://www.prnewswire.com/news-releases/seventy-percent-of-employees-unhappy-with-career-opportunities-300178571.html

Chamorro-Premuzic, T., & Furnham, A. (2010). *The psychology of personnel selection*. Cambridge: Cambridge University Press. doi:10.1037/h0052197

Chamorro-Premuzic, T., Winsborough, D., Sherman, R. A., & Hogan, R. (2016). New talent signals: Shiny new objects or a brave new world? *Industrial and Organizational Psychology*, 9(3), 621–640. doi:10.1017/iop.2016.6

Clayton, N., Williams, M., & Howell, A. (2014). Unequal opportunity: How jobs are changing in cities. Retrieved from https://www.centreforcities.org/publication/unequal-opportunity-how-jobs-are-changing-in-cities/

Coughlin, M. (2018). Zillow Group drives inclusion with augmented writing. Retrieved from https://textio.com/blog/zillow-group-drives-inclusion-with-augmented-writing/13035166577

Dastin, J. (2018). Amazon scraps secret AI recruiting tool that showed bias against women. Retrieved from https://www.reuters.com/article/us-amazon-com-jobs-automation-insight-idUSKCN1MK08G

Davison, K. K., Bing, M. N., Kluemper, D. H., & Roth, P. L. (2016). Social media as a personnel selection and hiring resource: Reservations and recommendations. In *Social media in employee selection and recruitment: Theory, practice, and current challenges* (pp. 15–42). doi:10.1007/978-3-319-29989-1_2

De Cooman, R., Gieter, S. De, Pepermans, R., Hermans, S., Bois, C. Du, Caers, R., & Jegers, M. (2009). Person-organization fit: Testing socialization and attraction-selection-attrition hypotheses. *Journal of Vocational Behavior*, 74(1), 102–107. doi:10.1016/j.jvb.2008.10.010

De Haan, R. (2018). Overcoming employment barriers facing underserved populations: 3 lessons. Retrieved from https://www.uschamberfoundation.org/blog/post/overcoming-employment-barriers-facing-underserved-populations-3-lessons

Derous, E., Buijsrogge, A., Roulin, N., & Duyck, W. (2016). Why your stigma isn't hired: A dual-process framework of interview bias. *Human Resource Management Review*, 26(2), 90–111. doi:10.1016/j.hrmr.2015.09.006

Derous, E., & Ryan, A. M. (2019). When your resume is (not) turning you down: Modelling ethnic bias in resume screening. *Human Resource Management Journal*, 29(2), 113–130. doi:10.1111/1748-8583.12217

Deshpande, K. V., Pan, S., & Foulds, J. R. (2020). Mitigating demographic bias in AI-based resume filtering doi:10.1145/3386392.3399569

Dvorak, N., & Pendell, R. (2018). Culture wins by attracting the top 20% of candidates. Retrieved from https://www.gallup.com/workplace/237368/culture-wins-attracting-top-candidates.aspx

Eurich, T. (2018). *Insight: The surprising truth about how others see us, how we see ourselves, and why the answers matter more than we think*. Currency.

Forbes Human Resources Council. (2017). 13 most common hiring process bottlenecks and how to correct them. Retrieved from https://www.forbes.com/sites/forbeshumanresourcescouncil/2017/07/11/13-most-common-hiring-process-bottlenecks-and-how-to-correct-them/?sh=2655e15f74d0

Golestani, A., Masli, M., Shami, N. S., Jones, J., Menon, A., & Mondal, J. (2018). Real-time prediction of employee engagement using social media and text mining. In 17th IEEE International Conference on Machine Learning and Applications (pp. 1383–1387). doi:10.1109/ICMLA.2018. 00225

Gosling, S. D., Ko, S., Mannarelli, T., & Morris, M. E. (2002). A room with a cue: Personality judgments based on offices and bedrooms. *Journal of Personality and Social Psychology*, 82(3), 379–398. doi:10.1037/0022-3514.82. 3.379

Guntuku, S. C., Lin, W., Carpenter, J., Ng, W. K., Ungar, L. H., & Preotiuc-Pietro, D. (2017). Studying personality through the content of posted and liked images on Twitter. In Proceedings of the 2017 ACM Web Science Conference (pp. 223–227). doi:10.1145/3091478.3091522

Hogan, R., & Bond, M. H. (2009). Culture and personality. In P. J. Corr & G. Matthews (Eds.), *The Cambridge handbook of personality psychology* (pp. 577–588). Cambridge University Press. doi:10.1017/CBO9780511596544.036

Jensen, J. M., & Patel, P. C. (2011). Predicting counterproductive work behavior from the interaction of personality traits. *Personality and Individual Differences*, 51(4), 466–471. doi:10.1016/J.PAID.2011.04.016

Joseph, J. (2016). *What companies use blind/anonymous resumes and what benefits have they reported?* Retrieved from https://ecommons.cornell.edu/xmlui/bitstream/handle/ 1813/74533/What_Companies_use_Blind_Anonymous_Res

umes_and_What_Benefits_Have_They_Reported.pdf?
sequence=1

Kern, M. L., McCarthy, P. X., Chakrabarty, D., & Rizoiu, M. A. (2019). Social media-predicted personality traits and values can help match people to their ideal jobs. *Proceedings of the National Academy of Sciences of the United States of America, 116*(52), 26459–26464. doi:10. 1073/pnas.1917942116

Kim, S. Y., & Song, H. Y. (2014). Predicting human location based on human personality. In *Lecture notes in computer science* (Vol. 8638, pp. 70–81). Cham: Springer. doi:10. 1007/978-3-319-10353-2_7

Kosinski, M., Stillwell, D., & Graepel, T. (2013). Private traits and attributes are predictable from digital records of human behavior. *Proceedings of the National Academy of Sciences, 110*(15), 5802–5805. doi:10.1073/pnas.1218772110

Kristof, A. L. (1996). Person-organization fit: An integrative review of its conceptualizations, measurement, and implications. *Personnel Psychology, 49*(1), 1–49. doi:10.1111/j. 1744-6570.1996.tb01790.x

Kuncel, N. R., Ones, D. S., & Sackett, P. R. (2010). Individual differences as predictors of work, educational, and broad life outcomes. *Personality and Individual Differences, 49*(4), 331–336. doi:10.1016/j.paid.2010.03.042

Landers, R., Brusso, R., & Auer, E. (2019). Crowdsourcing job satisfaction data: Examining the construct validity of glassdoor.com ratings. *Personnel Assessment and Decisions, 5*(3). doi:10.25035/pad.2019.03.006

Mann, A., & Harter, J. (2016). The worldwide employee engagement crisis. Retrieved from https://www.gallup.com/

workplace/236495/worldwide-employee-engagement-crisis.aspx

Matz, S. C., Kosinski, M., Nave, G., & Stillwell, D. J. (2017). Psychological targeting as an effective approach to digital mass persuasion. *Proceedings of the National Academy of Sciences*. 201710966. doi:10.1073/pnas.1710966114

Matz, S. C., Menges, J. I., Stillwell, D. J., & Schwartz, H. A. (2019). Predicting individual-level income from Facebook profiles. *PLoS ONE, 14*(3), e0214369. doi:10.1371/journal.pone.0214369

Maurer, R. (2015). Internal recruitment critical to hiring, retention. Retrieved from https://www.shrm.org/resourcesandtools/hr-topics/talent-acquisition/pages/internal-recruitment-critical-hiring-retention.aspx

Mayew, W. J., & Venkatachalam, M. (2012). The power of voice: Managerial affective states and future firm performance. *The Journal of Finance, 67*(1), 1–43. doi:10.1111/j.1540-6261.2011.01705.x

Melchers, K. G., Roulin, N., & Buehl, A. K. (2020). A review of applicant faking in selection interviews. *International Journal of Selection and Assessment, 28*(2), 123–142. doi:10.1111/ijsa.12280

de Montjoye, Y.-A., Quoidbach, J., Robic, F., & Pentland, A. (2013). Predicting personality using novel mobile phone-based metrics. In International Conference on Social Computing, Behavioral-Cultural Modeling, and Prediction (pp. 48–55). doi:10.1007/978-3-642-37210-0_6

Nature. (2018). Cambridge Analytica controversy must spur researchers to update data ethics. *Nature, 555*(7698), 559–560. doi:10.1038/d41586-018-03856-4

Nucleus Research. (2021). Talent acquisition reduces turnover by up to 60 percent. Retrieved from https://nucleusre search.com/research/single/talent-acquisition-reduces-turnover-by-up-to-60-percent/

O'Neil, C. (2016). *Weapons of math destruction: How big data increases inequality and threatens democracy.* Crown.

Ones, D. S., & Viswesvaran, C. (1998). The effects of social desirability and faking on personality and integrity assessment for personnel selection. *Human Performance, 11*(2–3), 245–269. doi:10.1080/08959285.1998.9668033

Pandey, S., & Pandey, S. K. (2019). Applying natural language processing capabilities in computerized textual analysis to measure organizational culture. *Organizational Research Methods, 22*(3), 765–797. doi:10.1177/1094428117745648

Pang, D., Eichstaedt, J. C., Buffone, A., Slaff, B., Ruch, W., & Ungar, L. H. (2020). The language of character strengths: Predicting morally valued traits on social media. *Journal of Personality, 88*(2), 287–306. doi:10.1111/jopy.12491

Park, G., Andrew Schwartz, H., Eichstaedt, J. C., Kern, M. L., Kosinski, M., Stillwell, D. J., … Seligman, M. E. P. (2015). Automatic personality assessment through social media language. *Journal of Personality and Social Psychology, 108*(6), 934–952. doi:10.1037/pspp0000020

Preoţiuc-Pietro, D., Lampos, V., & Aletras, N. (2015). An analysis of the user occupational class through Twitter content. *Proceedings of the 53rd Annual Meeting of the Association for Computational Linguistics and the 7th International Joint Conference on Natural Language Processing, 1,* 1754–1764. doi:10.3115/v1/P15-1169

Purkiss, S. L. S., Perrewé, P. L., Gillespie, T. L., Mayes, B. T., & Ferris, G. R. (2006). Implicit sources of bias in employment interview judgments and decisions. *Organizational Behavior and Human Decision Processes*, *101*(2), 152–167. doi:10.1016/j.obhdp.2006.06.005

Rad, M. S., Martingano, A. J., & Ginges, J. (2018). Toward a psychology of Homo sapiens: Making psychological science more representative of the human population. *Proceedings of the National Academy of Sciences of the United States of America*, *115*(45), 11401–11405. doi:10.1073/pnas.1721165115

Rothmann, S., & Coetzer, E. P. (2003). The big five personality dimensions and job performance. *SA Journal of Industrial Psychology*, *29*(1), 68–74. doi:10.4102/sajip.v29i1.88

Sajjadiani, S., Sojourner, A. J., Kammeyer-Mueller, J. D., & Mykerezi, E. (2019). Using machine learning to translate applicant work history into predictors of performance and turnover. *Journal of Applied Psychology*, *104*(10), 1207–1225. doi:10.1037/apl0000405

Saks, A. M. (2006). Antecedents and consequences of employee engagement. *Journal of Managerial Psychology*, *21*(7), 600–619. doi:10.1108/02683940610690169

Sambandam, S. (2019). The new age of automation in the recruitment process. Retrieved from https://www.hrtechnologist.com/articles/recruitment-onboarding/the-new-age-of-automation-in-the-recruitment-process/

Sandy, C. J., Gosling, S. D., & Durant, J. (2013). Predicting consumer behavior and media preferences: The comparative validity of personality traits and demographic variables.

Psychology and Marketing, 30(11), 937–949. doi:10.1002/mar.20657

Schmidt, F. L., & Hunter, J. E. (1998). The validity and utility of selection methods in personnel psychology: Practical and theoretical implications of 85 years of research findings. *Psychological Bulletin, 124*(2), 262–274. doi:10.1037/0033-2909.124.2.262

Schmitt, N. (2014). Personality and cognitive ability as predictors of effective performance at work. *Annual Review of Organizational Psychology and Organizational Behavior, 1*(1), 45–65. doi:10.1146/annurev-orgpsych-031413-091255

Schwartz, A. H., Eichstaedt, J. C., Dziurzynski, L., Kern, M. L., Seligman, M. E. P., Ungar, L. H., … Stillwell, D. (2013). Toward personality insights from language exploration in social media. *AAAI Spring Symposium Series*, 72–79. Retrieved from https://www.aaai.org/ocs/index.php/SSS/SSS13/paper/viewPaper/5764

Shami, N. S., Muller, M., Pal, A., Masli, M., & Geyer, W. (2015). Inferring employee engagement from social media. In Conference on Human Factors in Computing Systems (pp. 3999–4008). doi:10.1145/2702123.2702445

Shukla, S., Adhikari, B., & Singh, V. (2015). Employee engagement-role of demographic variables and personality factors. *Amity Global HRM Review, 5*(May), 65–73. Retrieved from https://www.researchgate.net/publication/316622110

Stachl, C., Au, Q., Schoedel, R., Gosling, S. D., Harari, G. M., Buschek, D., … Bühner, M. (2020). Predicting personality from patterns of behavior collected with smartphones. *Proceedings of the National Academy of Sciences of the*

United States of America, *117*(30), 17680–17687. doi:10.1073/pnas.1920484117

Sun, J., Schwartz, H. A., Son, Y., Kern, M. L., & Vazire, S. (2020). The language of well-being: Tracking fluctuations in emotion experience through everyday speech. *Journal of Personality and Social Psychology*, *118*(2), 364–387. doi:10.1037/pspp0000244

Swider, B. W., & Zimmerman, R. D. (2010). Born to burnout: A meta-analytic path model of personality, job burnout, and work outcomes. *Journal of Vocational Behavior*, *76*(3), 487–506. doi:10.1016/j.jvb.2010.01.003

Tausczik, Y. R., & Pennebaker, J. W. (2010). The psychological meaning of words: LIWC and computerized text analysis methods. *Journal of Language and Social Psychology*, *29*(1), 24–54. doi:10.1177/0261927X09351676

Textkernel. (2021). How CCL cut costs and reduced its sourcing time by 50% in Bullhorn. Retrieved from https://www.textkernel.com/how-ccl-cut-costs-and-reduced-its-sourcing-time-by-50/

The School of Life. (2016). Emotional technology - YouTube. Retrieved from https://www.youtube.com/watch?v=5u45-x0-zoY

Trindel, K., Polli, F., & Glazebrook, K. (2020). Using technology to increase fairness in hiring. Retrieved from https://www.umass.edu/employmentequity/sites/default/files/WhatWorks4_UsingTechnologytoIncreaseFairnessinHiring.pdf

Turczynski, B. (2021). Lying on a resume (2020 study). Retrieved from https://resumelab.com/resume/lying

Wang, Y., & Kosinski, M. (2018). Deep neural networks are more accurate than humans at detecting sexual orientation from facial images. *Journal of Personality and Social Psychology*, *114*(2), 246–257. doi:10.1037/pspa0000098

Westerman, J. W., & Cyr, L. A. (2004). An integrative analysis of person-organization fit theories. *International Journal of Selection and Assessment*, *12*(3), 252–261. doi:10.1111/j.0965-075X.2004.279_1.x

Woods, A., & Tharakan, S. (2021). *Hiring for diversity: The guide to building an inclusive and equitable organisation*. John Wiley & Sons.

Yam, J., & Skorburg, J. A. (2021). From human resources to human rights: Impact assessments for hiring algorithms. *Ethics and Information Technology*. doi:10.1007/s10676-021-09599-7

Young, H. R., Glerum, D. R., Wang, W., & Joseph, D. L. (2018). Who are the most engaged at work? A meta-analysis of personality and employee engagement. *Journal of Organizational Behavior*, *39*(10), 1330–1346. doi:10.1002/JOB.2303

Youyou, W., Kosinski, M., & Stillwell, D. (2015). Computer-based personality judgments are more accurate than those made by humans. *Proceedings of the National Academy of Sciences*, *112*(4), 1036–1040. doi:10.1073/PNAS.1418680112

5

GAMIFICATION AND GAME-BASED ASSESSMENTS

Serious games or game-based assessments are gaining popularity as an alternative to traditional psychometric assessments, which are based on simple questionnaires developed for pen and paper formats (Lumsden, Skinner, Woods, Lawrence, & Munafò, 2016; Quiroga, Román, De La Fuente, Privado, & Colom, 2016). This is unsurprising, given that games promise a better user experience, shorter assessment times, and potentially better quality and quantity of data. Indeed, compared to traditional psychometric tests, interactive assessments are more engaging and satisfying for respondents, and gamified quizzes are experienced as fun, enjoyable, and rewarding (Downes-Le Guin, Baker, Mechling, & Ruyle, 2012; Hamari, Koivisto, & Sarsa, 2014; Landers & Callan, 2011).

Game-based assessments can cover a variety of formats, from immersive computer game–like experiences to simple changes to questionnaire formats that increase interactivity or use experience. The latter are more common in recruitment and selection. Game-based assessments that look to replace psychometric tests used for employee selection are typically modeled after traditional psychometric tests but introduce levels of gamification. Gamification refers to the inclusion of elements commonly found in games such as direct feedback, level progression, increasing difficulty, intermittent goals, and, in the context of game-based psychometric assessments, the use of mobile online technology (Landers & Callan, 2011).

Much of the literature on game-based assessments focuses on cognitive ability, which is assessed with puzzles or "right or wrong" type questions that lend themselves well to game-based formats. Some attempts have been made to gamify personality tests, using images as well as storytelling. These attempts are promising but include less of the gamified elements used in cognitive ability games. Another avenue for testing personality without the use of questionnaires are personality assessment focused on video interviewing and language-based assessment of personality, which are described in Chapter three of this book.

Gamification of psychometric tests is the introduction of modern technology to psychometric test formats. The psychometric tests still prevalent today were designed before the wide availability of computers and the Internet. Their designs are therefore simple and suitable for pen and paper administration. This technical restriction in the design of psychometric tests has fundamentally shaped the way in which psychometricians not only measure but also define individual differences in cognitive ability, personality, and other traits. Many of the statistical and psychometric methods developed over the past decades are designed for data obtained from questionnaires and solve unique challenges resulting from this format. The field both in application and research has become reliant on the use of questionnaire-based tools. However, it is important to remember that questionnaires were the results of technical restrictions, and that the availability of modern technology provides an opportunity to rethink how we define and measure individual differences constructs. This requires innovation not only in assessment formats but also in scoring and statistical methods to evaluate tests, and an openness of the field as well as practitioners to embrace new types of tests. One example is the use of game-based assessment data to predict job performance directly. This is different from the use of traditional psychometric tests that measure specific traits and abilities, which are in turn linked to job performance. The data structure and technical characteristics of modern game-based assessments lend these assessments to custom scoring where data collected during the assessment is used to directly predict job performance. This strategy maximizes predictive validity with job performance data and might therefore exaggerate assessment performance when compared with traditional tests. Little is known about the generalizability of such models, which will be prone to sampling bias unless developed on large and diverse samples. Direct prediction scoring models also offer little transparency into the skills and traits that affect high or low performance on the assessment. At the same time, direct prediction has the potential to increase the benefit of prehire assessments and help identify the most talented applicants. Psychometric standards are needed to ensure they measure work relevant skills, and their performance can be compared to other tests.

Game-based assessments available today are only a starting point for what is possible. For example, intelligence can be predicted from video games, even when they were not designed to assess intelligence (Quiroga et al., 2016), and that personality can be inferred from a range of behavioral data (Chamorro-Premuzic, Akhtar, Winsborough, & Sherman, 2017). The challenge for psychometric test developers will be to imagine interactive formats that can serve to collect behavioral data and at that are at the same time suitable for employee selection in application from an ethical and practical standpoint.

GAMIFICATION ADVANTAGES

Game-based assessments for use in recruitment and selection are new and much of the literature on game-based assessment describes games used for specific populations (children, students, cognitively impaired), or in nonrecruitment contexts like marketing, education, or heath. Still, these studies offer valuable insights into the mechanisms through which gamification might improve or change the user experience, as well as showing examples of how tasks can be gamified. Game features such as real-time feedback, progression through levels, and clear goals result in an engaging user experience and feelings of flow, with some evidence that these benefits of games are retained when applied to game-based assessments or serious games (Burgers, Eden, Van Engelenburg, & Buningh, 2015; Chen, 2007; Connolly, Boyle, MacArthur, Hainey, & Boyle, 2012). For example, in populations with cognitive impairments, serious games to assess cognitive ability enhance the user experience and increase user enjoyment and satisfaction (Tremblay, Bouchard, & Bouzouane, 2010; Tso, Papagrigoriou, & Sowoidnich, 2015, p. 40). Game-based formats may also help in reframing selection tests as challenges. This framing helps reduce stereotype threat and anxiety (Alter, Aronson, Darley, Rodriguez, & Ruble, 2010). Cognitive ability tests tend to suffer from group differences, or adverse impact, in application some of which has been attributed to anxiety, motivation, or stereotype threat (Alter et al., 2010; McPherson & Burns, 2008). The framing of cognitive ability tests as games might help increase motivation and reduce stereotype threat and anxiety and thereby result in lower levels of group differences. Similarly, framing tasks as games increases interest and enjoyment (Lieberoth, 2015). Game-based formats can also help keep the attention of test takers, which might improve the quality of collected data (Klein, Hassan, Wilson, Ishigami, & Mulle, 2017).

By contrast, traditional assessments are typically long and can offer poor test-taker experience by making individuals feel stressed and not motivated (Tlili, Essalmi, Jemni, Kinshuk, & Chen, 2016). Traditional psychometric assessments are associated with poor respondent engagement (Krosnick, 1991). A main promise of game-based assessments is that through a combination of improving engagement, reducing fatigue, and shortening assessment times, they may enable comprehensive testing of several constructs. Questionnaire fatigue is a notorious problem with traditional formats (Krosnick, 1991). Several questions are needed to reliably assess a given trait or construct, and as a result assessments are often limited by their length, or the attention span of test takers, in application. This presents a challenge in the recruitment context where companies seek to select on a variety of traits, competencies, and abilities to identify top talent. This typically includes cognitive ability as well as personality tests. Indeed, although cognitive ability is the most consistent predictor of job performance, the highest predictive power is achieved when combining cognitive ability tests with other forms of assessment like personality tests (Schmidt & Hunter, 1998; Schmidt, Oh, & Shaffer, 2016). When combined, personality and cognitive ability offer the most valid predictions of job performance (Leutner & Chamorro-Premuzic, 2018). Both measure unique aspects of job performance and have incremental validity over each other in predicting job performance (Chamorro-Premuzic & Arteche, 2008; Judge, Higgins, Thoresen, & Barrick, 1999; Roberts, Kuncel, Shiner, Caspi, & Goldberg, 2007). It is therefore recommended to assess both personality and cognitive ability in the recruitment context. Using traditional assessments, this places considerable strains on job applicants, with long assessments times that often require the application process to be split into several stages.

If game-based assessments can reduce test times or increase engagement and thereby the tolerance of test takers, they might help reduce the steps needed in a recruitment process while delivering a comprehensive assessment of candidates. In addition to improvements in user experience, behavioral data collected from games offer a promising area for new types of psychometric assessments. By applying machine learning algorithms to large numbers of data points collected during gameplay, game-based assessments promise accuracy with shorter assessment time. This makes them particularly suitable to deliver comprehensive assessments of several characteristics such as personality and cognitive ability within a reasonable assessment time.

Game-based assessments promise an improvement of traditional psychometric tests using game technology and machine learning–based scoring algorithms. However, these assessment formats are new and while they are gaining traction in the applied context, the research literature is sparse. The following provides an overview of game-based assessments described in the academic literature. It provides an overview of the status of validation, and the scientific evidence available for the psychometric properties of game-based assessments of cognitive ability and personality.

GAME-BASED ASSESSMENTS FOR MEASURING COGNITIVE ABILITY: THE SCIENCE

Game-based assessments for cognitive ability, also called serious games in the research literature, are the best researched type of game-based assessments. Plenty of academic studies demonstrate that traditional cognitive ability or intelligence tests can be replicated or improved by implementing them in a game-based design. This is not surprising: cognitive ability tests typically include a series of puzzles or questions with right or wrong answers, and this translates well into game formats. Different levels of difficulty for a given task can be programmed automatically to generate easier or harder puzzles to solve. Cognitive ability is then gaged from a players' ability to solve harder puzzles. Making use of adaptive level progression, the level of difficulty can be adjusted to the ability of the candidate. This is also common in other adaptive psychometric tests and can help to shorten assessment times further (Green, Bock, Humphreys, Linn, & Reckase, 1984).

Cognitive ability tests might also enjoy the greatest benefit from gamification compared to, for example, personality test. Although cognitive ability has high predictive validity for job performance (Schmitt, 2014; Schmidt & Hunter, 1998; Schmidt et al., 2016), the user experience for job applicants is problematic. Traditionally long and strenuous cognitive ability tests may deter applicants, induce anxiety, or disadvantage those with test taking anxiety. The tradeoff between predictive validity and user experience means cognitive ability test use is typically restricted to high stakes job applications where applicants are willing to invest considerable time. By lifting the user experience and shortening testing times, game-based versions of cognitive ability tests open possibilities for lower stakes roles to benefit from the predictive validity of cognitive ability. For higher stakes roles, the improved user experience might present an advantage for competitive employers and help deter less candidates from the application process and improve employer image.

Several game-based assessments for cognitive ability are described and validated in the literature (Atkins et al., 2014;

Gamberini, Cardullo, Seraglia, & Bordin, 2010; Jimison, Pavel, McKanna, & Pavel, 2004; Verhaegh, Fontijn, Aarts, & Resing, 2013) with evidence that intelligence is accurately measured via games, or game-based assessments (Atkins et al., 2014; Luft, Gomes, Priori, & Takase, 2013; McPherson & Burns, 2008; Quiroga et al., 2015, 2016). This lays the foundation for game-based assessments used in industry. Cognitive ability describes a variety of intercorrelated mental skills. Although believed to have a genetic basis, cognitive ability is mostly conceptualized operationally as the ability to perform on a given psychometric assessment (Chamorro-Premuzic, 2011). As such, cognitive ability tests describe the test taker's maximum performance on a range of cognitive tasks. Originally developed to detect learning needs of young school children (Thorndike, Hagen, & Sattler, 1986), cognitive ability predicts a wide range of real world outcomes such as educational attainment, socioeconomic status, and career success (Schmidt & Hunter, 2004). Consequently, cognitive ability tests are used extensively today in education, health care, and talent identification (Chamorro-Premuzic, Von Stumm, & Furnham, 2015).

Game-based assessments of cognitive ability have been successfully developed for use in various settings as more engaging alternatives to questionnaire-based assessments (Jimison et al., 2004, 2007; Verhaegh et al., 2013). For example, the Great Brain Experiment validates a series of traditional cognitive tasks in gamified format on a smartphone in a large sample (Brown et al., 2014). Several other game-based assessments of intelligence are described in the literature: Gameplay across 12 separate short video games is highly correlated with cognitive ability in a sample of 188 university students ($r = 0.93$, $p < 0.01$; Quiroga et al., 2015). In a similar vein, a gamified four-dimensional spatial task predicts performance on several cognitive tasks in the general population, the highest correlations being found for working memory span tasks ($r = 0.62$, $p < 0.05$), quantitative reasoning tasks ($r = 0.30$, $p < 0.05$), and Raven's progressive matrices ($r = 0.37$, $p < 0.05$; Atkins et al., 2014). Gamified versions of working memory and processing speed tasks also correlate with traditional cognitive ability tests, including the Wechsler Adult Intelligence scales (correlations between gameplay and cognitive ability tests between $r = 0.54$, $p < 0.01$ and $r = 0.25$, $p < 0.05$; McPherson & Burns, 2008).

Predicting Real World Outcomes Using Cognitive Ability Game-Based Assessments

Although concurrent validity is important, the primary purpose of psychometric assessments is to offer a characterization of users that is related to a real-life outcome of interest, such as job performance, academic achievement, or clinical impairment (Chamorro-Premuzic, 2011). Thus, game-based assessments are useful only if they relate to real world outcomes in the same way that traditional psychometric assessments do. There is preliminary evidence that this is the case in relation to game-based assessments for cognitive ability (Luft et al., 2013; McPherson & Burns, 2008).

Several game-based assessments of cognitive ability demonstrate predictive validity in relation to real world outcomes, or even outperform traditional tests. Two game-based assessments of processing speed and working memory achieved higher correlations with academic performance than traditional tests (e.g., $r = 0.35$, $p < 01$ for the game-based assessments, compared with $r = 0.28$, $p < 0.05$ for the traditional test; McPherson & Burns, 2008). An artificial neural network successfully predicted low school achievement in mathematics from a game-like cognitive task, differentiating between students with typical and low school achievement (AUC = 0.897, Luft et al., 2013).

GAME-BASED ASSESSMENTS FOR PERSONALITY: THE SCIENCE

Several meta-analyses spanning decades of research demonstrate the predictive validity of the Big Five personality traits for job performance (Barrick & Mount, 1991; Higgins, Peterson, Pihl, & Lee, 2007; Hurtz & Donovan, 2000; Judge et al., 1999). Personality is assessed, in research and practice, with self-report questionnaires. The Likert scale used in early personality assessments, with answers ranging from opposing statements like "strongly disagree" to "strongly agree" is still dominant in personality testing today. Its prevalence and simplicity have operational advantages: questionnaires can be easily implemented online through preexisting survey platforms or readily available website templates, they are easy to score on a spreadsheet or with simple code, psychometricians are familiar with the format that fits into industry standards for statistical analyses and tests, users are familiar with answer formats, and, importantly, they work well in terms of reliability and validity. In addition, because Likert scale type personality test is so common, users have significant choice when selecting providers. Personality tests are available with different traits measured, interfaces, languages, feedback types, integrations, validation documentation, product features, and so on. Even free and open source Big Five tests are readily available, including norming pools, from the International Personality Item Pool (Goldberg, 1992).

However, self-report, Likert scale personality tests are prone to social desirability bias (Donovan, Dwight, &

Schneider, 2014), and due to their length can result in questionnaire fatigue and incomplete or invalid responses (Yan, Conrad, Tourangeau, & Couper, 2011). In seeking to resolve these issues, format innovations in the last decades have led to the development of new answer types as an alternative to the Likert scale. Forced choice questionnaires present a set of statements, typically each indicative of one of the traits measured. The choice of one item over the others provides information not only on the chosen traits but also the remaining traits as well. This shortens test times (Brown, 2010). Initially resulting in fixed totals such that a test taker could not rank high on all traits measured at the same time, innovations in scoring algorithms have made it possible to derive continuous scores from forced choice tests (Brown & Maydeu-Olivares, 2011). Forced choice tests reduce faking, or socially desirable answers, by making it harder to simply select a high score for each question (Guenole, Brown, & Cooper, 2018). This is particularly useful in high stakes settings where socially desirable faking occurs frequently (Arthur, Glaze, Villado, & Taylor, 2010). Adaptive testing applied to personality tests, where questions are displayed in response to users answering styles, has helped reduce testing times for personality tests (Forbey & Ben-Porath, 2007). Game-based assessment formats similarly reduce participants' ability to fake socially desirable answers (Montefiori, 2016).

Yet, forced choice tests keep the static format of questionnaires that is increasingly at odds with modern technology and user expectations. Game-based assessments offer a way to transport personality test formats into the 21st century by creating dynamic user interactions and shortening testing time. Indeed, the popularity of game-based assessments has risen in recent years (Chamorro-Premuzic et al., 2017; Winsborough & Chamorro-Premuzic, 2016), including in assessing personality. Unlike cognitive ability tests personality tests do not have a right or wrong answer. Personality instead measures behavioral tendencies and preferences. There are no wrong answers, only differences between people. This presents challenges for a gamification, where progression is often based on performance and game dynamics are created through increasing difficulty. In addition, the questionnaire-based format of traditional personality test does not directly translate into gamifiable puzzles like cognitive ability tests do. Practical implications placed an additional constraint on game-based personality assessments: Any game developed must improve the user experience and ideally shorten testing times. In contrast to cognitive ability test, the user experience of personality test is not anxiety inducing and as a result the pressure to change the format is lower. It is focused around shortening testing times and improving user experience and employer image, rather than resolving a pain point for applicants.

Perhaps for the reasons detailed above descriptions of game-based personality assessments are rare in the academic literature. These tend to fall into either games, storytelling approaches, or image-based tests.

Personality Tests as Games

Few games to measure personality are described in the literature, however, several personality games are described by assessment providers. These games typically present scenarios or situations where player behavior is measured and then used to predict the respective traits. Some of the games described by assessment providers resemble tasks designed for experimental psychology, decision-making, or economics research, calling their theoretical validity into question. One example is The Balloon Analogue Risk Task where players take varying risks to inflate a balloon without breaking it (Lejuez et al., 2002). These tasks are not designed to predict work relevant behaviors, or even to measure individual differences but to study cognitive processes or group dynamics. This means that scientific evidence for their relationship to job performance is limited or nonexistent. While they are developed by psychologists to measure human behaviors, they might not be suitable to predict the real world outcomes relevant in recruitment unless carefully matched to specific job tasks and locally validated. Nonetheless, given that personality describes behavioral tendencies and preferences, there is a theoretical foundation that gameplay behavior, if it measure behavioral tendencies, could be indicative of personality. Validity data and peer-reviewed publications describing the games are needed. Ventura and Shute describe a game-based assessment that measures persistence based on performance on Newtons Playground, a computer game where players complete a series of logical challenges based on qualitative physics. Performance on the games correlated moderately with an existing measure of persistence ($r = 0.22$; Ventura & Shute, 2013).

Gamification of Personality: Storytelling

One avenue taken to gamify personality tests is storytelling, adopting a strategy commonly used in situational judgment tests, a common assessment format: Scenarios are presented in an enriched environment that offers higher fidelity (i.e., similarity to the work environment) and increased engagement compared with questionnaires (Gkorezis, Georgiou, Nikolaou, & Kyriazati, 2021). McCord, Harman, and Purl (2019) describe a scenario-based game assessment to measure personality. The assessment consists of a fantasy game where players need to make a series of decisions to advance through the game. Gamification is introduced through the rich game environment and the fictitious storyline that players navigate. Available gameplay options are mapped onto the Big Five personality traits and personality scores are calculated based on the answers provided. This game achieves moderate convergent validity with traditional measures of personality and provides an example of how personality test questions might be presented in an engaging and interactive way (from $r = 0.20$ for openness to experience to $r = 0.48$ for neuroticism). However, in application the rich game context means that testing time is not shorter compared to traditional measures. Leutner, Codreanu, Liff, and Mondragon (2020) describe a similar approach for measuring emotion management. The game looks like a typical mobile phone messenger app, where players have a conversation with a fictitious colleague. Responses sent to the colleague indicate higher or lower levels of emotion management. This game again has moderate convergent validity with traditional questionnaire-based measures of emotion management ($r = 0.39$).

This scenario-based assessment of personality might increase user engagement and reduce fatigue and boredom. The enriched scenarios do however have a downside. Assessment time is unlikely to be reduced compared to traditional questionnaire-based assessments, and the large amount of text makes the assessments difficult to translate for use in an international context.

Gamification of Personality: Images

Alternative options for gamifying personality tests to the storytelling approach described above are images. Images can help capture and communicate rich context without requiring reading. This can reduce test taking time. Gaining traction in application, the literature on image-based personality test is scarce. One exception is the Red Bull Wingfinder assessment (Leutner, Yearsley, Codreanu, Borenstein, & Ahmetoglu, 2017). It includes an image-based assessment of personality described in the peer-reviewed literature. The assessment uses images to replace the Likert scale. Short statements are followed by a series of images from which participants select the image that most applies to them. A machine learning algorithm is used to predict personality based on the selected images. The image-based measure shows moderate convergent validity with curiosity, openness to experience and cognitive flexibility ($r = 0.35$ to $r = 0.52$), as well as test-retest reliability ($r = 0.62$ to $r = 0.65$). While this assessment includes a measure of openness to experience, there is a lack of studies describing image-based assessments of all Big Five traits. It is also not language agnostic, requiring translation of the question stems if used in other languages.

The language agnostic nature of images, in application, might be the biggest advantage of image-based personality test at least for international employers. Images are language agnostic, which has practical advantages for international application (Paunonen, Jackson, & Keinonen, 1990), meaning assessments do not need to be translated into separate target languages (Zhang, Zhang, Sang, & Xu, 2017). This does not necessarily do away with the need of validating an assessment in different cultures, as images might be interpreted differently across cultures, but it does alleviate the burden of translation. An example of a language agnostic personality test using images is described by Krainikovsky, Melnikov, and Samarev (2019). Instead of using the typical Likert scale used in personality test questionnaires to rate statements, the researchers used a bank of 300 images expressing different emotions and behaviors and showing a variety of scenarios and objects. Each image was tagged to describe its content. Respondents had to choose 20 to 100 images out of the image bank. Based on the image selection, a machine learning algorithm was used to predict Big Five personality scores with moderate convergent validity (mean validity $r = 0.25$; Krainikovsky et al., 2019). In application, this measure requiring respondents to look at 300 images would result in little time savings compared to questionnaire-based personality tests. However, the test is truly language agnostic and shows that image-based assessment formats can measure personality with some level of validity without requiring language. Note that this measure was not developed as a psychometric test for use in application or tested for reliability or validity.

Another example of a language agnostic test is provided by Paunonen, Ashton, and Jackson (2001) who used video scenarios instead of images to measure personality. Respondents view scenarios played out with stick-figures engaging in activities designed to display various levels of the Big Five personality traits. Respondents then rated the likelihood that they themselves would engage in the activity. The scenarios achieved moderate convergent validity with the Big Five (between $r = 0.45$ for neuroticism and $r = 0.59$ for agreeableness; Paunonen et al., 2001).

Games for Personality: The Best Way to Measure Personality?

There is an intuitive validity to the idea that image-based personality tests are more engaging compared to questionnaire-based test. However, this has not been tested or described in the academic literature. Any user experience gains will depend on the exact implementation of the image-based test. The same is true for game-based assessments of personality that use rich environments or storytelling. They run the risk of unnecessarily increasing test taking time and negating any user experience gains made from the engaging storyline. Alternative answer formats such as forced choice tests and even intuitive user interface designs of Likert scales implemented for mobile phone use present practical options for improving the user experience of personality tests, without the need to use a gamified test. Another alternative for measuring personality without personality questionnaires is the use of video interview assessments or analytics, or the use of free text to predict personality. The threshold for providers to offer valid, practical game-based personality assessments is therefore high.

SUMMARY OF PRACTICAL IMPLICATIONS

Standardized assessments of personality and intelligence are the most robust and valid method available for finding top talent in a pool of applicants at scale. Still, their application in the recruitment market is limited.

Game-based assessments remove significant barriers to the adoption of standardized assessments, thereby allowing more companies to benefit from their advantages: They deliver a high quality candidate experience, leading to less candidate drop out. They help improve the employer image compared with traditional self-report assessments, both because they are more engaging and because they are delivered on modern platforms, and in modern design. Most importantly, they cut assessment times dramatically, allowing recruiters to test attributes such as IQ in a matter of minutes, compared to lengthy traditional assessments that can take close to an hour.

Game-based assessments are new, and few providers can offer peer-reviewed studies to demonstrate their validity and reliability. This introduces a level of risk to HR practitioners who are tasked with choosing assessment providers. However, out of the new assessment methods described in this book, game-based assessments modeled after traditional assessments can readily be evaluated using standard psychometric principles. Their innovation value lies in the improved format and user experience. More complexity is introduced where games differ significantly from tasks included in traditional assessments or are linked directly to job performance rather than measuring an underlying trait. In this case, the leap from traditional assessments is greater, and a better understanding of how and why they work is needed to establish confidence that they are valid and reliable tools for detecting talent.

REFERENCES

Alter, A. L., Aronson, J., Darley, J. M., Rodriguez, C., & Ruble, D. N. (2010). Rising to the threat: Reducing stereotype threat by reframing the threat as a challenge. *Journal of Experimental Social Psychology*, *46*(1), 166–171. doi:10.1016/J.JESP.2009.09.014

Arthur, W., Glaze, R. M., Villado, A. J., & Taylor, J. E. (2010). The magnitude and extent of cheating and response distortion effects on unproctored internet-based tests of cognitive ability and personality. *International Journal of Selection and Assessment*, *18*(1), 1–16. doi:10.1111/j.1468-2389.2010.00476.x

Atkins, S. M., Sprenger, A. M., Colflesh, G. J. H., Briner, T. L., Buchanan, J. B., Chavis, S. E., … Dougherty, M. R. (2014). Measuring working memory is all fun and games. *Experimental Psychology*, *61*(6), 417–438. doi:10.1027/1618-3169/a000262

Barrick, M. R., & Mount, M. K. (1991). The big five personality dimensions and job performance: A meta-analysis. *Personnel Psychology*, *44*(1), 1–26. doi:10.1111/j.1744-6570.1991.tb00688.x

Brown, A. (2010). Doing less but getting more: Improving forced-choice measures with item response theory. *Assessment and Development Matters*, *2*(1), 21–25. Retrieved from https://kar.kent.ac.uk/44768/1/Brown2010 DoingLessButGettingMore.pdf

Brown, A., & Maydeu-Olivares, A. (2011). Item response modeling of forced-choice questionnaires. *Educational and Psychological Measurement*, *71*(3), 460–502. doi:10.1177/ 0013164410375112

Brown, H. R., Zeidman, P., Smittenaar, P., Adams, R. A., McNab, F., Rutledge, R. B., & Dolan, R. J. (2014). Crowdsourcing for cognitive science–The utility of smartphones. *PLoS One*, *9*(7), e100662. doi:10.1371/journal. pone.0100662

Burgers, C., Eden, A., Van Engelenburg, M. D., & Buningh, S. (2015). How feedback boosts motivation and play in a brain-training game. *Computers in Human Behavior*, *48*, 94–103. doi:10.1016/J.CHB.2015.01.038

Chamorro-Premuzic, T. (2011). *Personality and individual differences* (2nd ed.). Hoboken, NJ: BPS Blackwell.

Chamorro-Premuzic, T., Akhtar, R., Winsborough, D., & Sherman, R. A. (2017). The datafication of talent: How technology is advancing the science of human potential at work. *Current Opinion in Behavioral Sciences*, *18*, 13–16. doi:10.1016/j.cobeha.2017.04.007

Chamorro-Premuzic, T., & Arteche, A. (2008). Intellectual competence and academic performance: Preliminary validation of a model. *Intelligence, 36*(6), 564–573. doi:10.1016/j.intell.2008.01.001

Chamorro-Premuzic, T., Von Stumm, S., & Furnham, A. (2015). *The Wiley-Blackwell handbook of individual differences*. Chichester: Wiley-Blackwell. doi:10.1002/9781444343120

Chen, J. (2007). Flow in games (and everything else). *Communications of the ACM, 50*(4), 31–34. doi:10.1145/1232743.1232769

Connolly, T. M., Boyle, E. A., MacArthur, E., Hainey, T., & Boyle, J. M. (2012). A systematic literature review of empirical evidence on computer games and serious games. *Computers and Education, 59*(2), 661–686. doi:10.1016/j.compedu.2012.03.004

Donovan, J. J., Dwight, S. A., & Schneider, D. (2014). The impact of applicant faking on selection measures, hiring decisions, and employee performance. *Journal of Business and Psychology, 29*(3), 479–493. doi:10.1007/s10869-013-9318-5

Downes-Le Guin, T., Baker, R., Mechling, J., & Ruyle, E. (2012). Myths and realities of respondent engagement in online surveys. *International Journal of Market Research, 54*(5), 613–633. doi:10.2501/ijmr-54-5-613-633

Forbey, J. D., & Ben-Porath, Y. S. (2007). Computerized adaptive personality testing: A review and illustration with the MMPI-2 computerized adaptive version. *Psychological Assessment, 19*(1), 14–24. doi:10.1037/1040-3590.19.1.14

Gamberini, L., Cardullo, S., Seraglia, B., & Bordin, A. (2010). Neuropsychological testing through a Nintendo Wii® console. *Studies in Health Technology and Informatics, 154*, 29–33. doi:10.3233/978-1-60750-561-7-29

Gkorezis, P., Georgiou, K., Nikolaou, I., & Kyriazati, A. (2021). Gamified or traditional situational judgement test? A moderated mediation model of recommendation intentions via organizational attractiveness. *European Journal of Work & Organizational Psychology*, *30*(2), 240–250. doi:10.1080/1359432X.2020.1746827

Goldberg, L. R. (1992). The development of markers for the big-five factor structure. *Psychological Assessment*, *4*(1), 26–42. doi:10.1037/1040-3590.4.1.26

Green, B. F., Bock, R. D., Humphreys, L. G., Linn, R. L., & Reckase, M. D. (1984). Technical guidelines for assessing computerized adaptive tests. *Journal of Educational Measurement*, *21*(4), 347–360. doi:10.1111/j.1745-3984.1984.tb01039.x

Guenole, N., Brown, A. A., & Cooper, A. J. (2018). Forced-choice assessment of work-related maladaptive personality traits: Preliminary evidence from an application of Thurstonian item response modeling. *Assessment*, *25*(4), 513–526. doi:10.1177/1073191116641181

Hamari, J., Koivisto, J., & Sarsa, H. (2014). Does gamification work? A literature review of empirical studies on gamification. In 2014 47th Hawaii international conference on system sciences (pp. 3025–3034). doi:10.1109/HICSS.2014.377

Higgins, D. M., Peterson, J. B., Pihl, R. O., & Lee, A. G. M. (2007). Prefrontal cognitive ability, intelligence, big five personality, and the prediction of advanced academic and workplace performance. *Journal of Personality and Social Psychology*, *93*(2), 298–319. doi:10.1037/0022-3514.93.2.298

Hurtz, G. M., & Donovan, J. J. (2000). Personality and job performance: The big five revisited. *Journal of Applied Psychology, 85*(6), 869–879. doi:10.1037/0021-9010.85. 6.869

Jimison, H. B., Pavel, M., Bissell, P., & McKanna, J. (2007). A framework for cognitive monitoring using computer game interactions. *Studies in Health Technology and Informatics, 129*(2), 1073–1077. Retrieved from http://www. ncbi.nlm.nih.gov/pubmed/17911880

Jimison, H. B., Pavel, M., McKanna, J., & Pavel, J. (2004). Unobtrusive monitoring of computer interactions to detect cognitive status in elders. *IEEE Transactions on Information Technology in Biomedicine, 8*(3), 248–252. doi:10. 1109/TITB.2004.835539

Judge, T. A., Higgins, C. A., Thoresen, C. J., & Barrick, M. R. (1999). The big five personality traits, general mental ability, and career success across the life span. *Personnel Psychology, 52*(3), 621–652. doi:10.1111/j.1744-6570. 1999.tb00174.x

Klein, R. M., Hassan, T., Wilson, G., Ishigami, Y., & Mulle, J. (2017). The AttentionTrip: A game-like tool for measuring the networks of attention. *Journal of Neuroscience Methods, 289*, 99–109. doi:10.1016/J.JNEUMETH.2017. 07.008

Krainikovsky, S., Melnikov, M. Y., & Samarev, R. (2019). Estimation of psychometric data based on image preferences. In Conference proceedings for education and humanities (pp. 75–82). WestEastInstitute. Retrieved from https://www.westeastinstitute.com/wp-content/uploads/ 2019/06/EDU-Vienna-Conference-Proceedings-2019.pdf# page=75

Krosnick, J. A. (1991). Response strategies for coping with the cognitive demands of attitude measures in surveys. *Applied Cognitive Psychology*, *5*(3), 213–236. doi:10.1002/acp. 2350050305

Landers, R. N., & Callan, R. C. (2011). Casual social games as serious games: The psychology of gamification in undergraduate education and employee training. In M. Ma, A. Oikonomou, & L. C. Jain (Eds.), *Serious games and edutainment applications* (pp. 399–423). London: Springer. doi:10.1007/978-1-4471-2161-9_20

Lejuez, C. W., Richards, J. B., Read, J. P., Kahler, C. W., Ramsey, S. E., Stuart, G. L., ... Brown, R. A. (2002). Evaluation of a behavioral measure of risk taking: The balloon analogue risk task (BART). *Journal of Experimental Psychology: Applied*, *8*(2), 75–84. doi:10.1037/ 1076-898X.8.2.75

Leutner, F., & Chamorro-Premuzic, T. (2018). Stronger together: Personality, intelligence and the assessment of career potential. *Journal of Intelligence*, *6*(4), 1–10. doi:10. 3390/jintelligence6040049

Leutner, F., Codreanu, S.-C., Liff, J., & Mondragon, N. (2020). The potential of game- and video-based assessments for social attributes: Examples from practice. *Journal of Managerial Psychology*. doi:10.1108/JMP-01-2020-0023

Leutner, F., Yearsley, A., Codreanu, S. C., Borenstein, Y., & Ahmetoglu, G. (2017). From Likert scales to images: Validating a novel creativity measure with image based response scales. *Personality and Individual Differences*, *106*, 36–40. doi:10.1016/j.paid.2016.10.007

Lieberoth, A. (2015). Shallow gamification: Testing psycho-logical effects of framing an activity as a game. *Games and Culture*, *10*(3), 229–248. doi:10.1177/1555412014559978

Luft, C. D. B., Gomes, J. S., Priori, D., & Takase, E. (2013). Using online cognitive tasks to predict mathematics low school achievement. *Computers & Education*, *67*, 219–228. doi:10.1016/J.COMPEDU.2013.04.001

Lumsden, J., Skinner, A., Woods, A. T., Lawrence, N. S., & Munafò, M. (2016). The effects of gamelike features and test location on cognitive test performance and participant enjoyment. *PeerJ*, *4*(7), e2184. doi:10.7717/peerj.2184

McCord, J. L., Harman, J. L., & Purl, J. (2019). Game-like personality testing: An emerging mode of personality assessment. *Personality and Individual Differences*, *143*, 95–102. doi:10.1016/j.paid.2019.02.017

McPherson, J., & Burns, N. R. (2008). Assessing the validity of computer-game-like tests of processing speed and working memory. *Behavior Research Methods*, *40*(4), 969–981. doi:10.3758/BRM.40.4.969

Montefiori, L. (2016). Game-based assessment: Face validity, fairness perception, and impact on employer's brand image. *Assessment & Development Matters*, *8*(2), 19–22.

Paunonen, S. V., Ashton, M. C., & Jackson, D. N. (2001). Nonverbal assessment of the big five personality factors. *European Journal of Personality*, *15*(1), 3–18. doi:10.1002/per.385

Paunonen, S. V., Jackson, D. N., & Keinonen, M. (1990). The structured nonverbal assessment of personality. *Journal of Personality*, *58*(3), 481–502. doi:10.1111/j.1467-6494.1990.tb00239.x

Quiroga, M. Á., Escorial, S., Román, F. J., Morillo, D., Jarabo, A., Privado, J., … Colom, R. (2015). Can we reliably measure the general factor of intelligence (g) through commercial video games? Yes, we can! *Intelligence*, *53*, 1–7. doi:10.1016/j.intell.2015.08.004

Quiroga, M. Á., Román, F. J., De La Fuente, J., Privado, J., & Colom, R. (2016). The measurement of intelligence in the XXI century using video games. *Spanish Journal of Psychology*, *19*, E89. doi:10.1017/sjp.2016.84

Roberts, B. W., Kuncel, N. R., Shiner, R., Caspi, A., & Goldberg, L. R. (2007). The power of personality: The comparative validity of personality traits, socioeconomic status, and cognitive ability for predicting important life outcomes. *Perspectives on Psychological Science*, *2*(4), 313–345. doi:10.1111/j.1745-6916.2007.00047.x

Schmidt, F. L., & Hunter, J. E. (1998). The validity and utility of selection methods in personnel psychology: Practical and theoretical implications of 85 years of research findings. *Psychological Bulletin*, *124*(2), 262–274. doi:10.1037/0033-2909.124.2.262

Schmidt, F. L., & Hunter, J. (2004). General mental ability in the world of work: Occupational attainment and job performance. *Journal of Personality and Social Psychology*, *86*(1), 162–173. doi:10.1037/0022-3514.86.1.162

Schmidt, F. L., Oh, I.-S., & Shaffer, J. A. (2016). *The validity and utility of selection methods in personnel psychology: Practical and theoretical Implications of 100 years*. doi:10.13140/RG.2.2.18843.26400

Schmitt, N. (2014). Personality and cognitive ability as predictors of effective performance at work. *Annual Review of Organizational Psychology and Organizational Behavior*, *1*(1), 45–65. doi:10.1146/annurev-orgpsych-031413-091255

Thorndike, R. L., Hagen, E. P., & Sattler, J. M. (1986). *Stanford Binet intelligence scale*. Chicago, IL: Riverside Publishing.

Tlili, A., Essalmi, F., Jemni, M., Kinshuk, & Chen, N. S. (2016). Role of personality in computer based learning. *Computers in Human Behavior*, 64, 805–813. doi:10.1016/J.CHB.2016.07.043

Tremblay, J., Bouchard, B., & Bouzouane, A. (2010). Adaptive game mechanics for learning purposes–Making serious games playable and fun. Proceedings of the 2nd international conference on computer supported education, 2, 465–470. doi:10.5220/0002855604650470

Tso, L., Papagrigoriou, C., & Sowoidnich, Y. (2015). *Analysis and comparison of software-tools for cognitive assessment* (p. 40). Retrieved from http://elib.uni-stuttgart.de/opus/volltexte/2015/10181/

Ventura, M., & Shute, V. (2013). The validity of a game-based assessment of persistence. *Computers in Human Behavior*, 29(6), 2568–2572. doi:10.1016/J.CHB.2013.06.033

Verhaegh, J., Fontijn, W. F. J., Aarts, E. H. L., & Resing, W. C. M. (2013). In-game assessment and training of nonverbal cognitive skills using TagTiles. *Personal and Ubiquitous Computing*, 17(8), 1637–1646. doi:10.1007/s00779-012-0527-0

Winsborough, D., & Chamorro-Premuzic, T. (2016). Talent identification in the digital world: New talent signals and the future of HR assessment. *People and Strategy*, 39(2), 28–31. Retrieved from https://info.hoganassessments.com/hubfs/TalentIdentification.pdf

Yan, T., Conrad, F. G., Tourangeau, R., & Couper, M. P. (2011). Should I stay or should I go: The effects of progress feedback, promised task duration, and length of questionnaire on completing web surveys. *International Journal of Public Opinion Research*, *23*(2), 131–147. doi:10.1093/ijpor/edq046

Zhang, H., Zhang, J., Sang, J., & Xu, C. (2017). A demo for image-based personality test. *Lecture Notes in Computer Science: MultiMedia Modelling*, *10133*, 433–437. doi:10.1007/978-3-319-51814-5_36

6

FUTURE OF RECRUITMENT

In recent years, there has been a great deal of attention to the potential misuses of new recruitment technologies, in particular AI (Wilson et al., 2021). Although these concerns are wide-ranging, they usually center around the inadvertent introduction or proliferation of biases, the mismanagement and loss of confidential or sensitive personal data, and the uncomfortable realization that we live in a surveillance economy where our privacy has been lost, or at least diluted (Shank, Graves, Gott, Gamez, & Rodriguez, 2019). In a way, it doesn't matter so much whether these problems emerge as a consequence of technical gaps in those tasked with deploying AI in recruitment, whether the issue is insufficient attention to moral considerations, or merely that they are overly focused on optimizing for business outcomes at the expense of harming certain candidates or job seekers. The critical point is that AI, like any new tool or technology, has the potential to introduce unfairness and suffering in job seekers and applicants, often in ways not understood by employers (Hohenstein & Jung, 2020).

To be sure, humans have a long and rich history of worrying about evil technologies, which can be documented clearly in science fiction novels and movies. Apocalyptic fears of cyborgs going rogue, synthetic creatures acquiring Frankenstein-like qualities, or dystopian Orwellian societies controlled by rogue algorithms and anarchic AI systems. As Stephen Pinker noted, these fears are largely unwarranted because there is a clear, though often misunderstood, difference between capabilities and motivations, which even applies to the realm of AI. So, just because a machine *can* do something it doesn't mean it *wants* to, and still humans will still have the ability to preprogram machines' objectives and intentions, it would be silly to ask them to wipe out humanity or even enslave it. For that to happen, a superordinate AI would need to exist who is interested in achieving this goal and that implies acquiring independent motives, values, and even personality. Not only are we far from this, it is conceptually and technically illogical to expect this to happen. Now, whether unethical *humans* may use AI to advance their own evil interests and harm other humans is a different story altogether. But if history has proved one thing, it is that humans have never really been too dependent on technology or innovation, let alone AI, to inflict suffering on their peers. Consider that the list of anthropogenic or man-made (yes, they are usually men) disasters, such as war, genocide, forced labor, slavery, and oppression, dwarfs the impact of even the most devastating natural disasters. We don't need AI to introduce or impose unethical and destructive scenarios to the world of work or indeed any area of life. Humans have managed this rather well even with the most rudimentary technologies, as well as on their own.

So, our starting assumption when we think about the ethics and unethics of future recruitment tools is the notion that technology, including AI, is never ethical or unethical: rather, it is the ethics and unethics of its consequences, especially vis-à-vis the intentions of humans deploying it, we should scrutinize and evaluate. Melvin Kranzberg once noted that "technology is neither good nor bad, nor is it neutral." Meaning, even if tech can't be ethical or unethical per se, it is rarely neutral because when you impact human life you will generally have positive and negative effects, and sometimes both at once. It is with this basic premise that we examine how novel recruitment technologies and tools may affect humans and what we can do to minimize negative effects and maximize positive effects. We structure this chapter around what we believe *ought to be* the most general principles for benevolent uses of new recruitment tools, highlighting what we see as positive ways to adopt AI and other methodologies, not least because they represent an improvement over the status quo, or at least a more promising alternative to it. We see these principles as opportunities, which imply we are not quite naive enough to take them for granted, or unaware of the obstacles we face to live up to these very opportunities. But we need to start with what should happen in order to not just spot but also stop that which should not.

1. *Benefits to job seeker*: The most important principle or dimension of our ethical framework is both commonsensical and complex. The commonsense part is that any new technology or tool deployed in the recruitment process should introduce a benefit to job seekers – in other words, job seekers should be better off if it is used than if it is not – and ideally they will reap significant benefits from this new tool over and above alternatives. It is also easy to understand what these benefits would normally entail, namely a more meaningful and rewarding job, a career upgrade, the ability to unleash and grow their potential, as well as the ability to understand their talents and potential more

clearly. In other words, are job seekers improving their career prospects because of the new tool that is used to recruit them?

Now the complicated part: *which* job seekers or *who* really benefits? By definition, recruitment is always about selection and rejection of candidates, so can we ever expect a tool to benefit those who are rejected? Clearly, it is not possible to make everyone's life or career prospect better, so are we optimizing for helping *most* people ("the greatest amount of good for the greatest number" as Jeremy Bentham and John Stuart Mill postulated), or is our goal to help those who have historically been less fortunate (a big goal of diversity and inclusion interventions)? Or perhaps we are focused on benefiting those who could add most value to the business, but this starts to depart from a job seeker-centric approach to be merely business-centric in focus, and therefore less of an ethical act, and simply a business decision.

And while business decisions are not necessarily unethical, they tend to generate ethical blind spots precisely because they don't put job seekers or candidates first: after all, organizations, and especially for-profit corporations, are predominantly interested in maximizing their own effectiveness rather than in making the world a better place, though their marketing narratives and external communications often suggest otherwise. Today, there is clearly a trend to reduce the difference between profits and ethics perhaps because the world has become a better place, so there is pressure on businesses to act ethically, which actually puts a business premium on good, prosocial behaviors and a tax or penalty on bad or selfish behaviors (Bidwell, Briscoe, Fernandez-Mateo, & Sterling, 2013). For example, if an organization has the choice between a recruitment tool that helps them select the best performing candidates but reduces the degree of diversity in their workforce, or one that enables them to achieve a balance between both (i.e., high-performing candidates that are diverse), the business case is intertwined with – and dependent of – the ethical impact. In that sense, a philosophical question that arises is whether we can still call a business "ethical" when they engage in ethical actions purely as a means to boosting profits. For example, is the intent or motive underpinning the desire to increase female representation in leadership roles still ethical when a company is focused purely on avoiding a bad rep, losing clients, or regulatory sanctions? Clearly, the desire to do the right thing is a purer altruistic or ethical motive than the pursuit of altruistic or ethical actions in order to impress, and ultimately benefit, from others – or are they less different than we think? We return to this question at the end of this chapter.

2. *Informed consent:* The second principle is an important booster to the first and mitigates its potential problems. Why? Because in the absence of clear-cut criteria to establish whether job seekers benefit from new technologies and to address the nuances pertaining the specific context or situation, as well as the question of "what individual do we mean?", we can simply empower individuals to decide (Fleming, 2021). In that sense, ensuring that there is a transparent transaction with candidates, where they are fully aware of the potential consequences of the recruitment process, and willingly opt-in because they have made the educated and rational choice to be examined or vetted by a potential employer or recruiter, takes care of most of the potential ambiguities (Yam & Skorburg, 2021). Note, this principle addresses even the ethical

reservations around tools that, at face value, may seem intrusive, scary, or "creepy."

For example, there has been much resistance to the use of face-scanning technologies, such as the video interview, for recruitment purposes (even though smartphone users are happy to sign into their phones with it, Facebook users seem happy to tag their own and friends' faces, and few Zoom users are aware of what may happen with years of video and voice data accumulated through back-to-back work meetings). To most people, simply mentioning face scraping technologies is reminiscent of Orwellian dystopias, digital dictatorships, and autocratic governments surveilling their citizens to control and harm them (Chamorro-Premuzic, 2020). However, if it were made clear to job candidates that their digital interview data would be subjected to algorithmic profiling, so that a potential recruiter or employer could better determine if they are a good fit for a given role or job, it can be clearly up to candidates to decide whether this method poses a risk and whether the potential benefits (getting the job) outweigh the downsizes. Incidentally, this is best evaluated vis-à-vis alternatives: for example, are there any risks created by digital interview technologies (and AI video recruitment) not incurred by partaking in a traditional interview process? We recall a recent article in *The Washington Post* that warned that "a face-scanning algorithm increasingly decides whether you deserve the job." Although they were referring to AI, their statement is equally applicable to another face-scanning algorithm, namely the human brain, which has historically determined whether someone gets a job or not, and alas with several known pitfalls: ignoring key indicators or signals of talent, such as integrity, curiosity, and intelligence, mistaking irrelevant or problematic traits for talent, such as confidence, charisma, or psychopathy, and being unable to ignore key demographic signals, such as gender, race, age, and social class. To be clear, we advocate for proper regulation and scrutiny of any new tool, not least because job applicants (and organizations) are often unable to evaluate complex new technologies with rigor. But in doing so the main outcome is still to increase the information needed to produce informed consent. As an example, consider the difference between signing up for Facebook and signing up for Facebook after understanding what happens to your data – to enable the latter, you need to have the ability and motivation to include a long list of uses and describe them in very simple, user-friendly ways. This often calls for independent regulators (Scherman, Ing, Goldenberg, & Ferguson, 2019).

3. *Confidentiality, anonymity, and data protection:* Even if our previous two principles are addressed, organizations should ensure that, wherever possible, they protect and preserve the confidentiality, anonymity, and data protection of candidates (Kazim & Koshiyama, 2020). Of course, in a standard recruitment process, hiring managers and recruiters will need to identify the specific candidates to understand their scores and profile, but the number of people who have access to this information should be limited, and the information should be kept only for the purposes of the recruitment process. In fact, applying the first two principles to this one, we should enable candidates to willingly choose to share and disclose recruitment-related information with the specified parties mostly because they perceive a benefit to it. This also means data should be erased or deleted once the assignment is over, and no other parties should be given access to the data later on, unless candidates agreed. Needless to say, this also implies preventing data breeches and hacks, such that any

information disclosed during the recruitment purpose is only used for that purpose and ceases to exist after that. If organizations or recruiters feel the need to reuse or recycle these data, it should be justified vis-à-vis candidates' benefit and approved or chosen by them through informed consent. Yet, even if they do agree to this, data should be protected and kept as confidential as possible. In some instances, recruitment data can be examined at the aggregate level while preserving the candidate's anonymity. For example, if companies were interested in testing whether X or Y tool predicts future performance, they will want to mine group-level data and should not be interested in identifying individuals (Wilson et al., 2021). Equally, if companies were interested in understanding whether X or Y variable is theoretically and empirically linked to certain organizational outcomes, such as engagement, turnover, or productivity, they can work with aggregate data to preserve individuals' anonymity (Shen, DeVos, Eslami, & Holstein, 2021).

4. *Feedback and self-awareness:* While not generally a main criterion for ethics, in our view it is ethical to return as much information as possible to candidates, irrespective of whether they were offered a job or not. In the old days of traditional assessment tools, feedback was too complex and high-touch to deliver in an automated fashion, and having a coach or recruiter debrief each job applicant was expensive and not scalable. However, technology and data science have reduced the costs to giving feedback to a wide range of candidates to nearly zero, in the sense that feedback can be automated, so there's no additional costs to providing it to millions of people if you have done it for one (except, of course, cloud computing servers). This provides a great opportunities for organizations to engage

in ethical behaviors with rejected or not selected candidates, explaining them how they evaluated them and why their particular scores or profile was deemed a poor fit with the role, or not as strong as other candidates. To be sure, rejected candidates may always challenge unhappy decisions and question whether the score or desired talent profile was indeed correct, but to the degree that organizations use validated tools, such as science-based assessments (with or without AI), they will also be able to address these concerns and defend their decision. And of course, being rejected for no reason or told that "there were others better than you" is neither satisfying nor ethical, especially compared to a transparent explanation of company's rationale. This leads to our fifth and final principle.

5. *Explainability:* Recent AI ethics framework tends to converge on an important dimensions, namely explainability (Atkinson, Bench-Capon, & Bollegala, 2020). We could apply this to any innovation in recruitment. Explainable AI or explainable data science implies that we should not just be content with predicting things – and understanding that if you get X you may get Y – but also understanding and explaining things (Koshiyama et al., 2021). So, predicting that someone will be a high or low performer if they are hired is useful, but in order to leverage this prediction in an ethical way, we also want to understand and explain *why* they will be in one category or another. This principle puts a limit to blackbox algorithms that fail to explain the recruitment process. For example, research has found that many physical properties of people's voice and speech, such as tonality, pitch, and volume, are predictive of future work performance, as well as positive team and organizational outcomes (Winsborough & Chamorro-Premuzic, 2016). However, many of these

signals are hard to interpret, which makes it impossible for recruiters (or candidates) to understand why they scored well or poorly on such evaluations. Equally, just because academic studies have shown that "liking" curly fries on Facebook is indicative of having a higher IQ doesn't mean we understand why or can use curly fries Likes in the recruitment process (Kosinski, Stillwell, & Graepel, 2013). In short, we should favor tools, signals, and methods that boost our understanding of what someone is like, rather than simply increasing the probability that they are the right candidate, not least because this will also help us explain our decision to them, and make a rational decision on why they should join or not (back to point 4).

Needless to say, none of these principles will be achieved unless the deployed tool or method is actually accurate (Chamorro-Premuzic & Furnham, 2010). This makes prediction a precondition – necessary, yet not sufficient – for any of the other principles. Historically, we (at least academics) obsessed a lot over accuracy, perhaps to the detriment of other important components of recruitment tools (e.g., cost, simplicity, scalability, user experience, etc.) (Chamorro-Premuzic, Winsborough, Sherman, & Hogan, 2016). Now that the barriers to entry to developing new recruitment tools and technologies are so low and that engineers and software developers with very little knowledge of assessment and organizational psychology over-index in the world of HR tech and human capital technologies, we risk going into the opposite direction: all style and no substance will sell more than no style and all substance. If you work in this space and are overwhelmed by the amount of shiny new objects and exciting looking tools, including seemingly futuristic and "funky" products, the only thing we can say is "watch out."

There is a lot of noise and not so many signals here. Just because anyone can publish content in YouTube doesn't mean YouTube content is worth consuming. In fact, the more stuff gets put there the lower the percentage of stuff that achieves certain quality. It's the same with recruitment tools. Companies focus on great user X and branding and tell a story that sounds appealing but beneath the marketing spiel there is often no evidence, data, or science. A good question to ask new tech vendors is where the evidence for accuracy is and if they simply produce in-house White papers or technical manuals including limited evidence ("120 students completed this tool and their scores correlated with this other tool") or dubious claims ("we can predict performance with 98% degree of accuracy"), they belong to the realm of shampoo commercials rather than serious recruitment tools. Ideally, tools would have been validated using established scientific parameters, and the evidence would have been published in credible academic sources, such as peer-reviewed journals. Anything else is as good as you are inclined to believe, unless you realize it doesn't work.

So, accuracy or the evidence-backed promise that the method in question works, in the sense that it predicts the desired outcome, is a *sine-qua-non* for ethical recruitment, and we lament to say that unfortunately there's just little evidence for the idea that clients are able to discern it (generally speaking), or that there's no chance for inaccurate tools to compete in the crowded market of recruitment technologies. Quite the opposite: we continue to hear even from sophisticated and savvy clients that they are very happy with tools we would consider totally rogue and bogus, as would any academic colleague with expertize in this space. The science-practice gap in this area is big, and there is a worrying sense that technology is actually widening it (Winsborough & Chamorro-Premuzic, 2013). Perhaps because when things get more complex, it is harder for people to distinguish between something that works and something that doesn't, and easier for vendors to deceive others, even if they are telling the truth according to them, because they are mostly deceived, or at least confused, themselves. The need to add clarity to the vetting process of novel recruitment tools has never been bigger mostly because of the proliferation of useless tools that on the surface look a lot like robust and data-driven tools. This is not particularly new or recent (Ones, Kaiser, Chamorro-Premuzic, & Svensson, 2017). If the HR world truly cared about accuracy, the Myers Briggs Type Indicator (MBTI) would not be the most popular assessment tool in the world, used even with senior executives.

Still, amidst all the confusion and chaos, there is light at the end of the tunnel. Why do we say this? Because despite the unpredictable shape and form that future recruitment tools may take – by definition, if you can predict something, then it is not innovation – we can be confident that the standard parameters to evaluate new tools will remain largely unchanged. Indeed, science-based diagnostic tools, whether psychometric assessments or other evaluation tools used in recruitment and personnel selection, have always been scrutinized based on some universal overarching principle parameters, such as reliability and validity. Broadly speaking, reliability concerns whether the tool measures the same attribute with sufficient fidelity and accuracy, which we can quantify by testing or assessing it at different points in time, or getting multiple assessors rating or evaluating the same trait or person. It's a bit like going on a scale to weigh yourself every day: your weight should not fluctuate too much from one day to the next, and by the same token your personality or intelligence scores should not change much from one job application to the next. If something is stable, we expect its measurement to be stable. And if something is expressed or manifested clearly, we expect different tools or raters to converge in their profiles of it. But, just because you always get the same measure doesn't mean you are measuring something relevant, or even what you think you are. This is where validity comes in: a tool or method is valid if it produces a score that is predictive of a relevant outcome or criteria. For example, you want a leadership assessment to produce high leadership performance, an integrity test to predict ethical and moral behavior (and low scores to produce the opposite), and creativity tests to predict creative behaviors, and so on. A statistical link between a score in any recruitment test and a subsequent event represent a measure of that same individual's future performance, is what gives us the confidence that the test works, no matter what form or shape the test or signal has.

These criteria are not only useful to examine individual tools or methods but also to compare them with each other. In fact, because reliability and validity can be quantified or estimated in *degrees*, we can evaluate how powerful and accurate X tool is compared to Y and Z. This simply requires putting the same group of people through the same tools or assessments, and then determining which bit of information from which particular tool or method is most predictive. Suppose we have different tests claiming to measure someone's career potential. One could be a personality assessment (questionnaire), the other a resume parsing tool (which scrapes your past achievements as reported in a resume), the other a video interview algorithm (which translates your video and speech activity into a score), and the other a traditional job interview.

We may expect that all of these approaches could provide a score on candidates' "ambition," even if it is expressed via different signals (e.g., you answer positively to questions about your motivation, have a resume that includes top educational credentials and an impressive career track record, and talk in confident terms about yourself and your aspirations in an interview). Mining all these data together can help us determine the degree to which the different measures overlap, in that they evaluate the same trait in the same way, or whether they may complement each other (for example, ambition could be the sum of all these ambition scores). Importantly, to appease the debate or competition about "my tool is better than yours," we can actually test which of these different measures most strongly and accurately predicts future behaviors and achievements related to ambition. In short, the statistical parameters to decide whether we use one method or another are well-established, and companies can be data-driven when they decide to use one tool or another, which is the minimum we can expect if they want to be ethical. Because there are few opportunities to be ethical if you have chosen to evaluate people in the wrong way, or you are missing out of better, clearer insights about a candidate (Chamorro-Premuzic, 2017).

Fortunately, there are also robust and well-validated protocols to ensure that recruitment tools don't harm disadvantaged job applicants, such as less privileged, poorer, disabled individuals, and those who belong to groups that have historically been the target of prejudice and discrimination (Hickman et al., 2021). This could include certain genders (usually women), ethnic groups (such as Hispanics and Blacks in the United States), age groups (more often older workers, but sometimes younger workers), and people from lower socioeconomic status (Barocas & Selbst, 2016). For many decades we have had not just statistical procedures, but also laws and regulations, that identify and prevent tools from being used when they have *adverse impact*, meaning that their use significantly decreases the representation of these protected classes (Hogan, Hogan, & Roberts, 1996). Note that adverse impact may occur even in the absence of measurement bias, simply because it captures preferences, behaviors, or past accomplishments that are less common in some groups than others, which can be extended to any trait or attribute. So, for example, when AI is deployed to detect if job applicants have engineering qualifications in their CVs, it should not surprise us that women will under-index among the shortlisted candidates. Likewise, if a machine learning algorithm is used to predict whether a candidate is likely to get promoted in a group or organization, such as tech firm, it should not surprise us that middle-aged white male engineers may over-index in its selection of candidates. This is not because the AI or algorithm is biased, or because the people programming them are trying to perpetuate toxic masculinity or the supremacy of middle-aged white male engineers in the status quo, but rather, because that is indeed what happens in that system or organization. In other words, if you don't deploy these tools, this will still happen, which means that the tools are simply exposing an existing preference or bias, as opposed to introducing it (Segrest Purkiss et al., 2006).

In fact, this type of bias – outcome bias – is a common problem underpinning many applications of AI to assessment and recruitment (Shen et al., 2021). AI and algorithms mostly learn to find patterns and identify covariations, which they then use to classify events and make predictions. But since most of the events we are interested in predicting in recruitment are contaminated by human subjectivity and, yes, bias and prejudice, it is hard to train any AI to predict fair and unbiased outcomes (Ajunwa & Schlund, 2020). For example, when people's success within a job, role, or organization is largely determined by how they are evaluated in that system, and that is a function not just of how they perform, but what their boss thinks of them, you can see the problem. A boss may be good at making unbiased judgments and evaluations of their employees' performance, but s/he may also be consciously or unconsciously biased against employees because of their gender, nationality, attractiveness, class, and values (Taylor, 2017). After all, bosses are just like any other human, in that they like some humans more than others – and not always for logical or morally defensible reasons. And of course, even when bosses are open minded, worried about being ethical and fair, and very experienced managers, they will manage employees who manage impressions, play politics, take credit for others' achievements and blame others for their mistakes, or simply may be working in many different places, countries, modalities, so how can we expect a single boss to get it right about her or his 10 employees, when they are operating in a complex and ambivalent environment in which their perceptions are best seen as opinions rather than reflections of reality? This is quite different from asking a human to code or classify an object as a tree or a lamppost, so that an AI GPS navigator can learn and apply. Rules about human behavior at work come from other humans interpreting and evaluating them, so the old rule of "garbage in-garbage out" still applies to our training of algorithms (Whelan & DuVernet, 2015).

In some instances, the outcome or performance measures may actually be quite accurate, yet there may still be biases in them, courtesy of society. For example, AI may successfully learn that more attractive salespeople sell more, and their outcomes are pretty clear cut: more money generated in sales. However, since selling involves connecting with clients, establishing trust and rapport, and being liked by them, we can see how physical attractiveness (as well as race and gender) may be conflated here. Should a bar owner hire unattractive bar tenders? Well, if s/he wants to make the world fairer and open up career opportunities to previously neglected candidates, then yes. But if s/he wants to boost sales, maybe not. Of course, perhaps the most attractive bar tenders are not the best bar tenders, in that they may be less friendly, less good at mixing cocktails, and less honest. Yet at the end they may still generate more sales for the bar owners. At times, the conflict between ethics and profits exists independently of the tools used to recruit people, and what is at stake is the moral priorities of business leaders, as well as the values and culture of the organization. One would hope that applying fairness and ethical principles to the selection process would not just optimize for diversity and inclusion but also create working environments that attract other diverse candidates and harness a corporate reputation for being a prosocial and moral environment, which may in turn create customer loyalty and boost business profits. But we cannot forget that when biases and prejudices are engrained in society, our ethical acts may only be appreciated by a small proportion of the public. For every brand like Patagonia, there are many like Amazon, Uber, and Facebook, which maintain loyal and committed customers despite numerous exposes, media and regulatory attacks, and a reputation that is archetypically greedy and ruthlessly selfish rather than altruistic and ethical. And of course, this makes their shareholders rich and happy, even if a minority of them put pressure to encourage and drive more ethical behaviors.

Likewise, consumers may be skeptical of organizations which tokenize diversity and turn ethical acts into a blatant marketing campaign. Evolutionary psychologists have a great term for this called *virtue signaling* (Kurzban, Burton-Chellew, & West, 2015): basically advertising certain acts or behaviors so you convey desirable character attributes or attractive traits through them. According to this view, more or less anything prosocial for-profit organizations do – and stakeholder capitalism altogether – are Machiavellian attempts to outperform your competitors and drive sales, brand engagement, and get a positive rep with customers. In turn, these customers may be using the same brands and products to *virtue signal* themselves. If you think of a Silicon Valley entrepreneur wearing a Patagonia fleece (which has become harder since Patagonia decided to drop the logo for eco-responsible reasons) we can infer one of two things: they are a nice person, or trying hard to appear as a nice person. Equally, a firm that announces that it will give workers unlimited holidays, flexibility on where and how they work, and perhaps also drop Ivy League qualifications as a requirement for their top jobs, may also be telling us that they are nice, or trying to seem nice. And this logic also applies to organizations that advertise demographic changes to the configuration of their boards, leadership teams, or talent pool. This view seems cynical and negative, and it is hard to disapprove or refute it. However, the good news is that we don't really need to do so. After all, who cares if true altruism doesn't exist, so long as people behave in altruistic ways? Consider the unusual habit many ruthless self-made billionaires (from Carnegie and Rockefeller to Gates and Soros) have shown for giving away much of their fortune for humanitarian or altruistic causes. Yes, perhaps this is still part of their narcissism disguised as prosocial virtue signaling, and perhaps they are competing with each other to see who comes closer to unleashing their God complex: but they are still putting their money to a good cause and doing good, whereas the majority of billionaires and millionaires remain rather stingy with their fortunes. Surely it is not more ethical to refrain from doing good, even if it means being honest and refrain from virtue signaling?

Ultimately, it doesn't matter so much why someone – a person or an organization – seems interested in attending to ethical factors and harness a reputation for prosocial rather than greedy or selfish. The important part is what they decide to do and what consequences that has on others. And of course, actions matter more than words. On this we should be grateful that technology has made it very easy to register and record not just what people and organizations say, but also what they do. If there is pressure from outside, or bottom-up scrutiny, to behave better, this will drive better behaviors inside out. In short, we should appreciate that social and public pressure will continue to put pressure on organizations to behave in ethical and moral ways, as without the motivation to do good we cannot realistically expect good acts. Recruitment, and its future, will be no exception. Organizations today are under more pressure to be fair, unbiased, and meritocratic in their recruitment processes. We are at the opposite end of the spectrum of where this all started, namely blatant and shameless nepotism and aristocratic privilege as the status quo, up until perhaps 100 years ago (and of course still rampant in much of the world). If we have not just the right tools, but also the right expertize and the right motivation, we can expect a fairer and better future for most and the progressive removal of unfair privileges for the few.

REFERENCES

Ajunwa, I., & Schlund, R. (2020). Algorithms and the social organization of work. In M. D. Dubber, F. Pasquale, & S. Das (Eds.), *The Oxford handbook of ethics of AI* (pp. 803–822). New York, NY: Oxford University Press. doi: 10.1093/oxfordhb/9780190067397.013.52

Atkinson, K., Bench-Capon, T., & Bollegala, D. (2020). Explanation in AI and law: Past, present and future. *Artificial Intelligence, 289*, 103387. doi:10.1016/j.artint. 2020.103387

Barocas, S., & Selbst, A. (2016). Big data's disparate impact. *California Law Review*, *104*(3), 671–732. doi:10.15779/Z38BG31

Bidwell, M., Briscoe, F., Fernandez-Mateo, I., & Sterling, A. (2013). The employment relationship and inequality: How and why changes in employment practices are reshaping rewards in organizations. *The Academy of Management Annals*, *7*(1), 61–121. doi:10.1080/19416520.2013.761403

Chamorro-Premuzic, T. (2017). *The talent delusion: Why data, not intuition, is the key to unlocking human potential*. London: Piatkus.

Chamorro-Premuzic, T. (2020). Can surveillance AI make the workplace safe? *MIT Sloan Management Review*, *62*(1), 13–15. Retrieved from https://sloanreview.mit.edu/article/can-surveillance-ai-make-the-workplace-safe/

Chamorro-Premuzic, T., & Furnham, A. (2010). *The psychology of personnel selection*. Cambridge: Cambridge University Press. doi:10.1037/h0052197

Chamorro-Premuzic, T., Winsborough, D., Sherman, R. A., & Hogan, R. (2016). New talent signals: Shiny new objects or a brave new world? *Industrial and Organizational Psychology*, *9*(3), 621–640. doi:10.1017/iop.2016.6

Fleming, M. N. (2021). Considerations for the ethical implementation of psychological assessment through social media via machine learning. *Ethics & Behavior*, *31*(3), 181–192. doi:10.1080/10508422.2020.1817026

Hickman, L., Bosch, N., Ng, V., Saef, R., Tay, L., & Woo, S. E. (2021). Automated video interview personality assessments: Reliability, validity, and generalizability investigations. *Journal of Applied Psychology*. doi:10.1037/apl0000695

Hogan, R., Hogan, J., & Roberts, B. W. (1996). Personality measurement and employment decisions. *American Psychologist, 51*(5), 469–477. doi:10.1037/0003-066X.51.5.469

Hohenstein, J., & Jung, M. (2020). AI as a moral crumple zone: The effects of AI-mediated communication on attribution and trust. *Computers in Human Behavior, 106,* 106190. doi:10.1016/j.chb.2019.106190

Kazim, E., & Koshiyama, A. (2020). The interrelation between data and AI ethics in the context of impact assessments. *AI and Ethics.* 0123456789. doi:10.1007/s43681-020-00029-w

Koshiyama, A., Kazim, E., Treleaven, P., Rai, P., Szpruch, L., Pavey, G., … Lomas, E. (2021). Towards algorithm auditing: A survey on managing legal, ethical and technological risks of AI, ML and associated algorithms. *SSRN Electronic Journal.* doi:10.2139/ssrn.3778998

Kosinski, M., Stillwell, D., & Graepel, T. (2013). Private traits and attributes are predictable from digital records of human behavior. *Proceedings of the National Academy of Sciences of the United States of America, 110*(15), 5802–5805. doi:10.1073/pnas.1218772110

Kurzban, R., Burton-Chellew, M. N., & West, S. A. (2015). The evolution of altruism in humans. *Annual Review of Psychology, 66,* 575–599. doi:10.1146/annurev-psych-010814-015355

Ones, D. S., Kaiser, R. B., Chamorro-Premuzic, T., & Svensson, C. (2017). Has industrial-organizational psychology lost its way? *The Industrial-Organizational Psychologist, 54*(4), 67–74. Retrieved from https://www.siop.org/Research-Publications/Items-of-Interest/ArtMID/19366/ArticleID/1550/Has-Industrial-Organizational-Psychology-Lost-Its-Way

Scherman, M., Ing, C., Goldenberg, A., & Ferguson, S. (2019). A framework for trustworthy AI: The EU's new ethics guidelines. Retrieved from https://www.mccarthy.ca/en/insights/blogs/snipits/framework-trustworthy-ai-eus-new-ethics-guidelines

Segrest Purkiss, S. L., Perrewé, P. L., Gillespie, T. L., Mayes, B. T., & Ferris, G. R. (2006). Implicit sources of bias in employment interview judgments and decisions. *Organizational Behavior and Human Decision Processes*, *101*(2), 152–167. doi:10.1016/j.obhdp.2006.06.005

Shank, D. B., Graves, C., Gott, A., Gamez, P., & Rodriguez, S. (2019). Feeling our way to machine minds: People's emotions when perceiving mind in artificial intelligence. *Computers in Human Behavior*, *98*, 256–266. doi:10.1016/j.chb.2019.04.001

Shen, H., DeVos, A., Eslami, M., & Holstein, K. (2021). Everyday algorithm auditing: Understanding the power of everyday users in surfacing harmful algorithmic behaviors (pp. 1–28). Retrieved from http://arxiv.org/abs/2105.02980

Taylor, B. (2017). Your human bias. Retrieved from https://www.linkedin.com/pulse/human-bias-benjamin-taylor/

Whelan, T. J., & DuVernet, A. M. (2015). The big duplicity of big data. *Industrial and Organizational Psychology*, *8*(4), 509–515. doi:10.1017/iop.2015.75

Wilson, C., Ghosh, A., Jiang, S., Mislove, A., Baker, L., Szary, J., Trindel, K., & Polli, F. (2021). Building and auditing fair algorithms: A case study in candidate screening. In Proceedings of the 2021 ACM conference on fairness, accountability, and transparency (pp. 666–677). doi:10.1145/3442188.3445928

Winsborough, D., & Chamorro-Premuzic, T. (2013). Consulting psychology in the digital era: Current trends and future directions. *Consulting Psychology Journal*, 65(4). doi:10.1037/a0035698

Winsborough, D., & Chamorro-Premuzic, T. (2016). Talent identification in the digital world: New talent signals and the future of HR assessment. *People and Strategy*, 39(2), 28. Retrieved from https://info.hoganassessments.com/hubfs/TalentIdentification.pdf

Yam, J., & Skorburg, J. A. (2021). From human resources to human rights: Impact assessments for hiring algorithms. *Ethics and Information Technology*, 2019. doi:10.1007/s10676-021-09599-7

7

THE FAR FUTURE (POSSIBILITIES BEYOND TOMORROW)

The task of recruitment and selection, put simply, is to find the right person for the right job, and the right job for the right person. As a field, we have made some progress toward developing methodologies, tools, and practices, including structured interviews, psychometric assessments, and guidelines for fairness and diversity to help make this happen. Data from academic studies and practical applications show that these methods work to help improve recruitment decisions (Hough & Oswald, 2000; Schmidt, Oh, & Shaffer, 2016). We have described new tools, like video-interviewing and talent signals, which lean on those established methodologies while making use of modern technology in the previous chapters of this book. We have also discovered some of the limitations of these tools as well as the technologies we have available today: a reliance on flawed job performance data, the need for extensive sampling, and a lack of data to link personality to specific jobs in a meaningful way. These limitations highlight the magnitude of the task at hand: finding the right person for the right job remains a challenge. Even more so, helping someone find their ideal job remains a challenge.

With the technology and data available today, the odds for solving this challenge have never been better. For the first time ever, data about people's jobs, their networks, and behaviors is widely available in a structured way, on platforms like Twitter and LinkedIn but also within companies. Where organizational psychologists for the last century were limited by the constraints of questionnaire research and tedious or costly data collection, the possibilities for obtaining data about the world of work are ripe today. Technology to analyze these data is also becoming more readily available, and researchers have done the groundwork in developing models that predict psychometric traits other attributes relevant to organizational and psychologists from a range of behavioral data. This means that data obtained from platforms like Twitter can be enriched with personality profiles without the need to obtain survey responses. Examples of research conducted in this way are starting to emerge in academic journals, and practitioners are adapting these technologies to develop new HR tools like video-interviewing with automated analysis (Hickman, Bosch, et al., 2021; Hickman, Saef, et al., 2021; Kern, McCarthy, Chakrabarty, & Rizoiu, 2019). With the extent and quality of data available, organizational psychologist may finally be able to answer some of the long-standing questions in the field: what personality profile is most suitable to what job roles? How can we structure job roles and professions in a way that is meaningful and might help people find a suitable career? What behaviors are indicative of job performance and how can we select for and encourage these behaviors?

At the same time, even with the best data and technology available, we can only build the world that we can imagine. Solving long-standing problems in the field is only part of the potential of technology. Technology can also help us define and solve previously unimaginable tasks. Therefore, when we look into the far future of recruitment, we should define the dreams that we have for our field. What problems do we want to solve? How can technology help us develop new tools to achieve these dreams? How can we reimagine selection so that it helps us build the future of work that we want?

The following sections will first look at some of the dreams and goals of organizational psychologists and the field of recruitment and selection, and then look at emerging technologies that might help build the future of recruitment and selection. It is not a prediction of what might be coming, but rather an invitation to reflect on the purpose of our work and imagine what might be possible using new technologies.

DREAMS AND POSSIBILITIES FOR RECRUITMENT AND SELECTION

Recruitment and selection are key drivers of company performance and economic growth (Ekwoaba, Ikeije, & Ufoma, 2015). Making the wrong recruitment decisions can be costly both in terms of loss productivity, replacement cost, as well as psychological well-being and productivity costs to existing employees (Boushey & Glynn, 2012). Missed recruitment opportunities can also be detrimental to company performance, in particular when recruitment results in a homogenous workforce: Diversity in the workforce results in significant business advantages (Hunt, Prince, Dixon-Fyle, & Yee, 2018). At the same time, on an individual level, job satisfaction and career success have a significant impact on well-being (Bowling, Eschleman, & Wang, 2010). This is not apprising given that working adults spend the largest proportion of their time at work (Thompson, 2016). Recruitment and selection therefore is also a key driver of well-being. The wrong person in the wrong job is not only detrimental to the employer but also to the employee. Recruitment decisions are consequential for individuals, for companies, and for society. They also occur frequently, with an upward tendency: employees from Generation Z are three times more likely to change jobs than their Baby Boomer counterparts (Heitmann, 2018). This is also true for career choices. 49% of people change their career within their working lives (Indeed, 2019). Equally, recruitment and selection decisions do not just occur at the job entry point. Internal project, client, responsibility, and team allocations, as well as promotion decisions, occur frequently throughout an employee's life span and have a significant effect on the organization's performance and make up, as well as, the individual's career progression and job satisfaction.

Given the wide-ranging impact of recruitment and selection decisions, what might we dream of achieving with recruitment and selection in an ideal world?

Meritocracy and Diversity

Finding the best person for a job remains the number one goal of recruitment and selection. But what do we mean when we say the best person for a job? Arguably, it is the person that is most skilled and talented, regardless of their background, age, ethnicity, or social class. Yet, today's workforce is starkly homogenous, particularly in terms of gender and ethnicity. This raises a red flag. Recruitment and selection practices seem to be consistently missing out on talent available in non-white, non-male groups (Cambridge Network, 2019). As a result, companies are not using the best talent available to them and instead competing in a limited pool of talent. This perpetuates existing systems of exclusion. Talented candidates will not be given the opportunity to develop their potential, and this prevents their socio economic advancement, as well as the diversification of organisations. Apart from ethical and moral concerns, the effective limiting of talent pools to specific genders and ethnicities has a detrimental effect on company performance. For example, organizations with gender diverse executive teams have a 34% higher return to shareholders than those without (Catalyst, 2004). Performance boosts in diverse teams might stem from the fact that they can be recruited from a larger talent pool, or on the reverse, that homogenous teams are limited by an unnecessarily narrow talent pool, and inevitably need to lower recruitment standards to fill positions.

Persistent gender and ethnic biases in today's workforce are certainly not a sole result of recruitment and selection practices. Wide-ranging societal and economic factors play a role. However, bias in recruitment and selection is ripe. Where hiring managers make decisions, the prevalence of biases is clear. A reliance on shortcuts and gut feeling lead to flawed and biased recruitment decisions (Dovidio, Gaertner, Kawakami, & Hodson, 2002). This is not surprising given that many recruitment decisions need to be made under time pressure and with limited information, both of which heightens the effect of human bias in decision-making (Macrae, Bodenhausen, & Milne, 1998). The same CV receives less job interview invitations when it is titled by a white sounding versus an ethnic minority name (Zschirnt & Ruedin, 2016). Job interviewers rate applicants differently depending on their ethnicity and gender. When evaluating members of a stereotyped group, individuals are more likely to interpret ambiguous information to confirm stereotypes (Hilton & Von Hippel, 1996) or make memory errors consistent with stereotypes (Eberhardt, Dasgupta, & Banaszynski, 2003). Decision-makers in organizational contexts associate attractiveness with competence in male but not female candidates (Lee, Pitesa, Pillutla, & Thau, 2015). Job roles and industries have strong gendered associations, with high-paying and highly qualified roles gendered male (Clarke, 2020). While biases in terms of ethnicity and gender are evident in the recruitment decisions made, this is less true for talent. It is often difficult if not impossible to evaluate the true quality of a recruitment decision in practice. Performance data are not available for those who are not hired into the role, and it is therefore impossible to a certain extent that the selected candidate was the right choice over other applicants. But there is reason to believe that recruitment decisions are just as flawed in terms of selecting the most competent candidates as they are in terms of diversity. Interviewers are subject to applicant impression management. Narcissistic or psychopathic applicants tend to make highly competent impressions on hiring managers because they engage in impression management, do not shy away from lying or exaggeration, and use their charm to win over interviewers (Paulhus, Westlake, Calvez, & Harms, 2013). These techniques are effective at making good impressions during interviewing but are detrimental to job performance and team compatibility. It also means that companies are missing out on talented individuals in favor of those who are good at impression management.

Structured interviews and the use of psychometric assessments that measure job relevant skills and attributes go some way toward reducing or remedying the human bias in recruitment and selection decision-making. Of the different selection methods commonly used today, such as experience, demographic info, work samples, and interviews, structured interviews as well as psychometric tests exhibit relatively low ethnic and gender bias (Schmidt & Hunter, 1998). They also correlate with job performance, providing some evidence that they help identify the most talented applicants (Ployhart & Holtz, 2008). Although they represent an improvement compared to gut feeling or shortcut-based decision-making in unstructured recruitment processes, these methods are not free of bias. Cognitive ability tests in particular present a problem, with consistent bias toward selecting white male applicants.

Professional guidelines generally permit the presence of low levels of bias, which are a practical inevitability, though it is debatable to which degree. No test will always score all groups in the same way. But this practically necessary allowance for differences can become a problem in practice where the bias is consistent toward the same groups throughout different steps in the recruitment process, as well as across the organizational and societal context. Minority applicants start out underrepresented in an application process, for example, because recruitment was focused on certain universities or geographic areas where minorities are less present, they then may be slightly less likely to pass a cognitive ability or other assessment compared to majority applicants, and finally they will face additional human bias if they progress to an interview. The bias of assessments like cognitive ability is often justified through the high predictive validity of job performance. However, job performance data itself are biased and recorded in organizations that are part of a homogenous world of work. Performance data are based on manager or coworker ratings which are subject to biases (Prendergast & Topel, 1993). Where job performance data are based on objective measures such as sales performance, it might still underestimate the talent and performance of minority employees who must contend with the challenges of working in an environment that is centered around the needs and views of others. In comparative studies, minority groups are consistently underestimated and undervalued, as a result of their skills being viewed only in relation to the skills of the minority group (Ahl & Marlow, 2012). Recruitment and selection procedures and assessments built for and with a majority group workforce will discount those who are not part of the majority group. This leads to a reinforcement of the homogenous workforce, where minority applicants are less likely to be selected.

To summarize, our goal of finding the right person for the job is obstructed by biases and a reliance on background or other information that obstructs ability. In addition, many of the assessment and selection tools available today were researched on and developed for a homogenous western, white, and male workforce. If we imagine a future that solves the "best person for the role" problem, it seems that we need to (1) find and increase the use of reliable measures and indicators of talent and (2) develop tools that take an inclusive and holistic approach to talent as well as measuring performance. We have seen recruitment processes that focus on competence and standardize decision-making improve hiring outcomes in terms of diversity and performance. The use of such tools needs to be extended, as well as improving the fairness of the tools themselves. Technology offers promising avenues to implement structured interviews and assessments in user-friendly and practical ways, as we've seen in the previous chapters of this book. At the same time, even when selection tools are in use, progress on diversity in organizations is slow. Selection tools can help stack of the odds for minority applicants but hiring and promotion decisions are ultimately human, made by managers and bosses who will reliably hire like for like (Prewett-Livingston, Veres, Feild, & Lewis, 1996). If bosses and managers are non-diverse, progress on diversity in the higher levels of management will be slow if happening at all. Equally, if diverse applicants are underrepresented, or do not enter the application process at all, no matter how fair the selection tool, it will not produce a diverse workforce. If selection processes keep modeling job performance that is designed for the current, homogenous workforce, applicants that are not represented in this workforce will continue to compare unfavorably and continue to be excluded.

In order to make real and faster progress toward a talent-based, diverse workforce, selection tools may need to be redesigned from scratch, with the technologies available today deployed to solve the problems outlined above. Here are some questions you might ask to start imagining this future:

- How useful are our current bias evaluation methods for assessments when they do not result in a diverse workforce? Should workforce diversity become the focus of adverse impact and fairness assessments for recruitment processes?

- When does selection and recruitment start? Is evaluating the fairness of candidate assessments enough? How fair are sourcing strategies, and how diverse is the applicant base?

- How are we defining and measuring job performance? Should we strive to recruit those who perform best in our current workforce, or in the diverse workforce of the future?

A Fulfilling Career

Before any job application comes a vision, or at least the decision, to try and work in a given field or role. For the most privileged, the options are plentiful and the decision to pursue a given career is not only a way to generate income but also to find fulfillment in life. A frequent question to an organizational psychologist is: What should I do? What am I good at? What work suits my skills and interests? Yet, as a field we have surprisingly few answers to provide, at least when we look at research that matches individuals to careers. Attempts have been made to classify common job roles into meaningful career categories (U.S. Department of Labor Employment and Administration Training, 2000) and to measure individual skills and career preferences (Armstrong, Day, McVay, & Rounds, 2008).

Some tools even attempt to put the two together and recommend specific job roles based on psychometric traits, preferences, or attitudes. Yet, job recommendation tools available today are severely limited, largely due to lack of data. To make empirically based recommendations, one would need data on the psychometric traits, preferences, and attitudes of people, their chosen career, as well as, in order to not just recommend a career where similar people might work but also a career where a person is likely to be most successful or satisfied, career success and satisfaction data. On career platforms and social networks like LinkedIn and Twitter, these data are, for the first time, available in a structured way and on a large scale. We might be closer than ever to providing individual evidence-based career advice.

Entering a profession has a huge impact on future earning potential, job satisfaction, career prospects, and ultimately life satisfaction. Getting the right people into the right roles will also boost company performance and economic output. Developing career advice or job matching tools, if they work, might be one of the most worthwhile endeavors for organizational psychologists in the coming decades.

- What does it take to determine which individuals are thriving in which jobs or industries?

- Can we use data available today to help shape careers and present opportunities based on individual characteristics and interests?

A (Psychologically) Safe and Productive Workplace

Recruitment and selection decisions shape organization. They influence the diversity and competence of the workforce,

which in turn contributes to company culture and performance. The influence of recruitment and selection decisions
does not stop at the point of hiring, nor are selection decisions
restricted to hiring decisions. Internal recruitment, promotions, and leadership allocations are all internal selection
decisions that usually impact the productivity of a company
and the well-being of its workforce. But many are informal
and taken frequently by decision-makers across the company.
Borrowing from what we know about unstructured selection
processes at the point of hiring and how they result in biased
decision-making, we can expect these informal decisions to be
especially vulnerable to missing out on talent. When structured and standardized processes are missing, and decision-
makers lack reliable information about talent, they are
vulnerable to making biased decisions based on background,
impression management or politics. For example, those who
speak most during meetings are more likely to emerge as
leaders, regardless of what they say, a phenomenon coined the
"Babble Hypothesis" (MacLaren et al., 2020).

Work should be about work, but complexity and politics,
in particular in larger organizations, obscure the relationship
between performance and perception thereof. Because performance and talent become difficult to observe, employees
can gain more from engaging in politics and creating an
impression that they are working hard than they can gain
from contributing to company performance (Podsakoff,
Mackenzie, & Hui, 1993). Impression management becomes
more important for career progression than productivity
(Cheng, Chiu, Chang, & Johnstone, 2014). At the same time,
the company loses out on top performers who are not
recognized as such and denied opportunities for career progression. The glass ceiling is not just a reflection of inequality
and biases, but also clear evidence that companies fail to make
internal recruitment and selection decisions based on talent

and productivity, rather relying on superficial criteria. The economic costs of the glass ceiling are well-documented (Schmid & Urban, 2018). Its effects on well-being and career satisfaction are also apparent: The glass ceiling increases women's intention to quit (Stewart, Volpone, Avery, & McKay, 2011), can lower women's self-esteem (Tran, 2014), and reduces the chances for female employees to build networks and support systems for their careers (Freeman, 1990). The glass ceiling reduces the well-being of women managers (Babic & Hansez, 2021). These effects are exacerbated for women of colour: McKinsey report that the small pipeline gains made by women along the corporate ladder between 2016 and 2021 have not translated into gains for women of colour (Krivkovich, Starikova, Robinson, Valentino, & Yee, 2021). A lack of recognition of talent in internal progression and selection decisions is alienating those groups of the workforce that are already underrepresented. This leads to a further narrowing of the talent pool as job levels increase (Menzies, 2019).

There is a clear productivity loss to the company, not just in selecting individuals who are good at politics versus good at their jobs, and by alienating and losing top performers, but also in the time and effort lost by individual employees who need to engage in self-promoting behaviors and experience reduced well-being. This is not just a problem for individuals and selection and promotion decisions but also for organizational performance and overall. There are significant productivity costs to scaling a workforce because as team and organization sizes go up, more time needs to be invested in project coordination, internal lobbying, and knowledge exchange (European Business Awards, 2017).

Internal recruitment and opportunity allocation, just as recruitment, should be focused on people's talents. Getting the most talented individuals into a company is only part of the work. Recognizing and promoting their talent and making sure that those who contribute are rewarded are essential for companies to get the best out of their talented workforce. It is also essential to create a workplace where well-being and job satisfaction are possible for employees in underrepresented groups. Burnout is higher in women compared to men across corporate job levels, indicating that women endure higher strain and more stressors than their male colleagues (Krivkovich et al., 2021). If selection tools can get better at measuring competence not just at the point of entry but throughout tenure in a company, they might help build a workforce that is structured around talent and competence, exposing the biased decision-making present in informal decision-making as well as providing reliable information to decision-makers.

- How are selection decisions and opportunity allocations made internally? Can these decisions be formalized?

- What information should organizational psychologists provide to decision-makers to help them promote based on competence?

- What practical and scalable tools could we design to better measure performance and infuse this information into decision-making across the company?

- How can companies change so that diverse talent feel comfortable working and using their talents there?

SELECTION AND RECRUITMENT TECHNOLOGIES OF THE FUTURE – POSSIBILITIES IMAGINED

The recruitment and selection landscape today is shaped by the technological constraints, and opportunities, of the past decades. Digitalization and the Internet have fundamentally changed how organizations connect with jobseekers and find employees, as well as how we connect with coworkers. Software applications have alleviated much of the administrative burden of the recruitment process for Human Resource departments and hiring managers. Equally, digitalization has taken away many of the logistic efforts in administering common selection procedures like psychometric assessments and job interviews. However, this technological progress largely creates more efficient versions of preexisting tools and processes. The time for more radical innovation has come: As we move from using digitalization to automate tedious processes toward using artificial intelligence and machine learning to enhance or make knowledge-based decisions, the potential for improving recruitment and selection is huge. The following is a list of interesting technology that has emerged in recent years as well as some technology that is already created but not uses that scale, technology that has been described in research, but is not used in practice, and potential technology applications that have not been developed.

Performance Management

With much of our work lives being conducted digitally, there is a whole new world of possibilities in tracking and analyzing how people work. On the more sinister side, this has already led to the development and application of employee surveillance tech. Companies are tracking online activity in what is a computerized version of presentism (Adams, 2021). It did not take long before ingenious methods for tricking activity trackers by using pets, robots, or kids to tap on keyboards had gone viral (Morse, 2021). This misses the point and potential of work behavioral data. But it also highlights the fact that recording and use of work behavior data comes at the significant cost of eroding employee privacy. We have seen the profound impacts that loss of privacy has had in the online advertising and social networking space.

At the same time, it is hard to ignore the potential of work behavior data to solve some of the long-standing problems in recruitment and selection, in particular issues with measuring performance and an over reliance on impressions over competence. If we imagine a standardized data-driven system that allocates projects, opportunities and promotions, this system can be monitored and adjusted for bias in a way decentralized human decision-making cannot. It might also, and this is an open question, be better at detecting performance and potential than human managers. This could help organizations use talent more effectively.

Job performance is the ultimate outcome measure in recruitment and selection. The validity and success of assessment tools and selection methods are evaluated against job performance. Yet our current tools for measuring performance are either reliant on costly and bias-prone evaluations from managers and coworkers in the form of 360 questionnaires, or, where they are objective, fail to be generalizable across roles and functions. Work behavioral data present an opportunity to rethink and redesign job performance measures. If they can be improved this will have far reaching effects on our ability to improve almost all aspects of selection and recruitment.

Matchmaking

One of the areas where the availability of job performance data might help improve recruitment and selection is matchmaking, matching people to jobs, careers, or teams. First, if we understand who performs well in which roles and careers, we can recommend similar people to go into the same areas. That's historically been a very difficult problem to solve, but data availability presents a real opportunity to make progress. A team of researchers was able to analyze the personalities of different professions, as well as those who show high-performance in their profession, based on Twitter data (Kern et al., 2019). For example, top software developers had higher levels of openness compared to lower ranking developers, but lower levels of conscientiousness extraversion (Kern et al., 2019). Second if we have a good understanding of the different skills available within an organization, we can match employees to projects. The same applies to contractors, consultants, or service providers.

The quality of matches will hugely depend on the available data. The challenge is to obtain a large and diverse enough dataset that contains performance and/or satisfaction, individual differences, and job role data. Twitter is just one example of where these data might be available. Social media, job search sites, and internal company data all contain structured data needed for matchmaking. The question is whether researchers will be able to access these data and whether companies will have an economic incentive to build data-driven matchmaking tools.

Rebalancing the Relationship between Employer and Candidate

Job search platforms and social media are commonplace today. They have helped companies connect with candidates as well as individuals connect within their industry. Still, the way in which we look for jobs has remained largely the same: companies put out job posts, applicants scan platforms and drop boards and apply to the roles they seem suitable. While job search sites and networks like LinkedIn do provide customized job post recommendations, these link back to the traditional job post. As a result, companies end up with large volumes of applicants, exacerbating the power in balance even further. Only a fraction of applicants get hired. The power imbalance in this relationship is striking. Often, candidates invest significant effort into their job applications, preparing CVs and application letters, signing up to application portals, confirming eligibility criteria, and completing assessments, for a minimal chance at success. This effort is replicated for each job application. Companies mandate the format in which candidates apply and often give away little information until the very last steps of the recruitment process. This is particularly true about the teams and people that an applicant would end up working with. The job application process is dehumanized. Compare this to the online dating world and imagine you would need to submit your life history and undergo automated tests before even finding out who you might end up on a date with.

The one-sided job application might be outdated by a more balanced and automated, data-driven process. Work-related data and social media platforms might enable us to create more active and selective recruitment processes that save the efforts of thousands of applicants with few prospects for getting hired, as well as save companies the effort to evaluate thousands of unsuitable applications. Even without these data that would help facilitate better matches before a job application is made, technology might help us rethink the application experience. Think about dating apps again: With a low effort, light touch experience, they pulled online dating from the sidelines to the center of today's dating world.

Work Automation and What We Will Look for in
Future Employees

Finally, in addition to new tools and technology, when we think about the future of recruitment and selection we should also consider what skills and abilities we might need to select for in the workplace of the future. Automation is fundamentally changing the way organizations work, taking away or at least reshaping many of the job roles and even professions that people work in today. This will lead to the emergence of new roles. It is impossible to predict what these roles might be, but we might consider which human skills are subject to automation. Automation is taking away the burden of administrative tasks and reduces the need for repetitive process-based roles (Ellingrud, 2018). But automation is not limited to such tasks. Machine learning and artificial intelligence systems can replicate complex human decision-making or work processes. Even deeply human roles like management might be automated in the future, with some companies already attempting this (e.g., Satalia; Andrew, 2018). Artificial intelligence can also support and enhance decision-making by providing additional knowledge and insight that would be impossible for humans to generate. In this case, rather than replacing human decision-making, technology complements and enhances the work of humans. For example, machine learning algorithms are helping physicians make diagnoses (Fatima & Pasha, 2017). What skills will remain uniquely human, and what human skills would be required to interact with tomorrow's technologies? Human creativity might be one of those human skills. With repetitive tasks and data-driven insights completed by algorithms, solving complex problems, imagining the future, and creating systems, products or tasks that previously did not exist might become the center of human work.

If we imagine that we can make automation work for us, we might also use it to increase job satisfaction. With human well-being in mind, the development of automation will be focused on tasks that humans experience as tedious or annoying. Automation has already increased economic productivity (Executive Office of the President, 2016). If we manage to share the wealth generated by this increase in productivity, automation might lead to shorter working weeks and more discretionary time. This in turn might increase the creativity, curiosity, and well-being of people who will have more autonomy over their time. It might also take away some of the stark economic burdens of work and enable more individuals to engage with work out of a sense of accomplishment and interest, rather than necessity.

REFERENCES

Adams, R. D. (2021). Employers are watching remote workers and they're monitoring these activities. *TechRe public*. Retrieved from https://www.techrepublic.com/article/employers-are-watching-remote-workers-and-theyre-monitoring-these-activities/

Ahl, H., & Marlow, S. (2012). Exploring the dynamics of gender, feminism and entrepreneurship: Advancing debate to escape a dead end? *Organization*, *19*(5), 543–562. doi: 10.1177/1350508412448695

Andrew, P. (2018). Nine ways artificial intelligence is changing how and where we work. *Corporate Real Estate Journal*, *8*(1), 84–99. Retrieved from https://www.ingentaconnect.com/content/hsp/crej/2018/00000008/00000001/art00007

Armstrong, P. I., Day, S. X., McVay, J. P., & Rounds, J. (2008). Holland's RIASEC model as an integrative framework for individual differences. *Journal of Counseling Psychology*, *55*(1), 1–18. doi:10.1037/0022-0167.55.1.1

Babic, A., & Hansez, I. (2021). The glass ceiling for women managers: Antecedents and consequences for work-family interface and well-being at work. *Frontiers in Psychology*, *12*, 677. doi:10.3389/fpsyg.2021.618250

Boushey, H., & Glynn, S. J. (2012). *There are significant business costs to replacing employees*. Center for American Progress. Retrieved from https://cdn.americanprogress.org/wp-content/uploads/2012/11/16084443/CostofTurnover0815.pdf

Bowling, N. A., Eschleman, K. J., & Wang, Q. (2010). A meta-analytic examination of the relationship between job satisfaction and subjective well-being. *Journal of Occupational and Organizational Psychology*, *83*(4), 915–934. doi:10.1348/096317909X478557

Cambridge Network. (2019). Older job applicants less likely to get an interview. Retrieved from https://www.cambridgenetwork.co.uk/news/559149

Catalyst. (2004). The bottom line: Connecting corporate performance and gender diversity. Retrieved from https://www.catalyst.org/wp-content/uploads/2019/01/The_Bottom_Line_Connecting_Corporate_Performance_and_Gender_Diversity.pdf

Cheng, J. W., Chiu, W. La, Chang, Y. Y., & Johnstone, S. (2014). Do you put your best foot forward? Interactive effects of task performance and impression management tactics on career outcomes. *The Journal of Psychology:*

Interdisciplinary and Applied, *148*(6), 621–640. doi:10.1080/00223980.2013.818929

Clarke, H. M. (2020). Gender stereotypes and gender-typed work. In K. Zimmerman (Ed.), *Handbook of labor, human resources and population economics* (pp. 1–23). Cham: Springer International Publishing. doi:10.1007/978-3-319-57365-6_21-1

Dovidio, J. F., Gaertner, S. L., Kawakami, K., & Hodson, G. (2002). Why can't we just get along? Interpersonal biases and interracial distrust. *Cultural Diversity and Ethnic Minority Psychology*, *8*(2), 88–102. doi:10.1037/1099-9809.8.2.88

Eberhardt, J. L., Dasgupta, N., & Banaszynski, T. L. (2003). Believing is seeing: The effects of racial labels and implicit beliefs on face perception. *Personality and Social Psychology Bulletin*, *29*(3), 360–370. doi:10.1177/0146167202250215

Ekwoaba, J. O., Ikeije, U. U., & Ufoma, N. (2015). The impact of recruitment and selection criteria on organizational performance. *Global Journal of Human Resource Management*, *3*(2), 22–33. Retrieved from http://196.45.48.59:8080/bitstream/handle/123456789/2423/Theimpactofrecruitmentandselectioncriteriaonorganizationalperformance.pdf?sequence=1&isAllowed=y

Ellingrud, K. (2018). The upside of automation: New jobs, increased productivity and changing roles for workers. Retrieved from https://www.forbes.com/sites/kweilinellingrud/2018/10/23/the-upside-of-automation-new-jobs-increased-productivity-and-changing-roles-for-workers/?sh=20b5f44e7df0

European Business Awards. (2017). Hurdles to growth–The company level challenges. Retrieved from https://www. businessawardseurope.com/download/EBA_Hurdles_to_ Growth_Research.pdf

Executive Office of the President. (2016). Artificial intelligence, automation, and the economy. Retrieved from http://www.retiredinvestor.com/resources/Research-Materi als/Economy/AI_and_Economy_Report.pdf

Fatima, M., & Pasha, M. (2017). Survey of machine learning algorithms for disease diagnostic. *Journal of Intelligent Learning Systems and Applications*, 9(1), 1–16. doi:10. 4236/jilsa.2017.91001

Freeman. (1990). *Managing lives: Corporate women and social change*. Amherst, MA: University of Massachusetts Press.

Heitmann, B. (2018). The job-hopping generation: Young professionals are on the move. Retrieved from https://blog. linkedin.com/2018/october/11/the-job-hopping-generation- young-professionals-are-on-the-move

Hickman, L., Bosch, N., Ng, V., Saef, R., Tay, L., & Woo, S. E. (2021). Automated video interview personality assessments: Reliability, validity, and generalizability investigations. *Journal of Applied Psychology*. doi:10.1037/apl0000695

Hickman, L., Saef, R., Ng, V., Woo, S. E., Tay, L., & Bosch, N. (2021). Developing and evaluating language-based machine learning algorithms for inferring applicant personality in video interviews. *Human Resource Management Journal*. doi:10.1111/1748-8583.12356

Hilton, J. L., & Von Hippel, W. (1996). Stereotypes. *Annual Review of Psychology*, 47(1), 237–271. doi:10.1146/ annurev.psych.47.1.237

Hough, L. M., & Oswald, F. L. (2000). Personnel selection: Looking toward the future—Remembering the past. *Annual Review of Psychology*, *51*(1), 631–664. doi:10. 1146/annurev.psych.51.1.631

Hunt, V., Prince, S., Dixon-Fyle, S., & Yee, L. (2018). *Delivering through diversity*. McKinsey & Company. Retrieved from http://sylviakern.com/wp-content/uploads/2019/10/Deliveri ng-through-diversity_full-report_KcKinsey_2018_Business Case_DIM2018-2.pdf

Indeed. (2019). *Career change report: An inside look at why workers shift gears*. Retrieved from https://www.indeed. com/lead/career-change

Kern, M. L., McCarthy, P. X., Chakrabarty, D., & Rizoiu, M. A. (2019). Social media-predicted personality traits and values can help match people to their ideal jobs. *Proceedings of the National Academy of Sciences of the United States of America*, *116*(52), 26459–26464. doi:10. 1073/pnas.1917942116

Krivkovich, A., Starikova, I., Robinson, K., Valentino, R., & Yee, L. (2021). Women in the Workplace 2021. McKinsey. Retrieved from https://www.mckinsey.com/featured-insi ghts/diversity-and-inclusion/women-in-the-workplace

Lee, S., Pitesa, M., Pillutla, M., & Thau, S. (2015). When beauty helps and when it hurts: An organizational context model of attractiveness discrimination in selection deci- sions. *Organizational Behavior and Human Decision Processes*, *128*, 15–28. doi:10.1016/j.obhdp.2015.02.003

MacLaren, N. G., Yammarino, F. J., Dionne, S. D., Sayama, H., Mumford, M. D., Connelly, S., … Ruark, G. A. (2020). Testing the babble hypothesis: Speaking time predicts leader emergence in small groups. *The Leadership Quarterly*, *31*(5), 101409. doi:10.1016/j.leaqua.2020.101409

Macrae, C. N., Bodenhausen, G. V., & Milne, A. B. (1998). Saying no to unwanted thoughts: Self-focus and the regulation of mental life. *Journal of Personality and Social Psychology*, *74*(3), 578–589. doi:10.1037/0022-3514.74.3.578

Menzies, F. (2019). Diversity & inclusion best-pratice: Inclusive recruitment. Retrieved from https://cultureplus consulting.com/wp-content/uploads/2019/11/Inclusive-Recruitment-3.pdf

Morse, J. (2021). How to keep your Slack status "active" while "working" from home. Retrieved from https://mashable.com/article/how-to-keep-slack-status-active-while-away

Paulhus, D. L., Westlake, B. G., Calvez, S. S., & Harms, P. D. (2013). Self-presentation style in job interviews: The role of personality and culture. *Journal of Applied Social Psychology*, *43*(10), 2042–2059. doi:10.1111/JASP.12157

Ployhart, R. E., & Holtz, B. C. (2008). The diversity-validity dilemma: Strategies for reducing racioethnic and sex subgroup differences and adverse impact in selection. *Personnel Psychology*, *61*(1), 153–172. doi:10.1111/j.1744-6570.2008.00109.x

Podsakoff, P. M., Mackenzie, S. B., & Hui, C. (1993). Organizational citizenship behaviors and managerial evaluations of employee performance: A review and suggestions for future research. *Research in Personnel and Human Resources Management*, *11*, 1–40. Retrieved from https://www.semanticscholar.org/paper/Organizational-

citizenship-behaviors-and-managerial-Podsakoff-MacKenz
ie/089479f1b11f68e582c451bca8371e8393c8070c

Prendergast, C., & Topel, R. (1993). Discretion and bias in performance evaluation. *European Economic Review*, *37*(2–3), 355–365. doi:10.1016/0014-2921(93)90024-5

Prewett-Livingston, A. J., Veres, J. G., Feild, H. S., & Lewis, P. M. (1996). Effects of race on interview ratings in a situational panel interview. *Journal of Applied Psychology*, *81*(2), 178–186. doi:10.1037/0021-9010.81.2.178

Schmidt, F. L., & Hunter, J. E. (1998). The validity and utility of selection methods in personnel psychology: Practical and theoretical implications of 85 years of research findings. *Psychological Bulletin*, *124*(2), 262–274. doi:10.1037/0033-2909.124.2.262

Schmidt, F. L., Oh, I.-S., & Shaffer, J. A. (2016). The validity and utility of selection methods in personnel psychology: Practical and theoretical Implications of 100 years. doi:10.13140/RG.2.2.18843.26400

Schmid, T., & Urban, D. (2018). The economic consequences of a 'glass-ceiling': Women on corporate boards and firm value. AFA 2016 San Francisco meetings paper. doi:10.2139/ssrn.2344786

Stewart, R., Volpone, S. D., Avery, D. R., & McKay, P. (2011). You support diversity, but are you ethical? Examining the interactive effects of diversity and ethical climate perceptions on turnover intentions. *Journal of Business Ethics*, *100*(4), 581–593. doi:10.1007/s10551-010-0697-5

Thompson, K. (2016). What percentage of your life will you spend at work? Retrieved from https://revisesociology.com/2016/08/16/percentage-life-work/

Tran, T. T. T. (2014). *Identifying the existence of the glass ceiling and examining the impact on the participation of female executives in the Vietnamese banking sector.* Master of business thesis. Unitec Institute of Technology. Retrieved from https://www.researchbank.ac.nz/handle/10652/2693

U.S. Department of Labor Employment and Administration Training. (2000). O*NET career exploration tools version 3.0. Retrieved from https://files.eric.ed.gov/fulltext/ED455450.pdf

Zschirnt, E., & Ruedin, D. (2016). Ethnic discrimination in hiring decisions: A meta-analysis of correspondence tests 1990–2015. *Journal of Ethnic and Migration Studies, 42*(7), 1115–1134. doi:10.1080/1369183X.2015.1133279

INDEX